Perspectives on Kentucky's Past

ARCHITECTURE, ARCHAEOLOGY, AND LANDSCAPE

Julie Riesenweber

General Editor

ROCK ART
OF
KENTUCKY

FRED E. COY, JR.

THOMAS C. FULLER

LARRY G. MEADOWS

JAMES L. SWAUGER

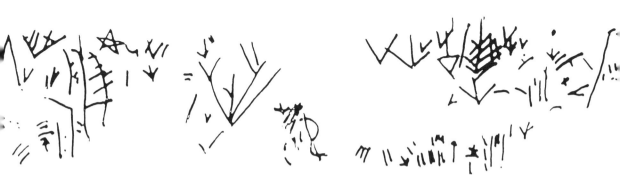

THE UNIVERSITY PRESS OF KENTUCKY

Publication of this volume was made possible in part by
a grant from the National Endowment for the Humanities.

Scholarly publisher for the Commonwealth,
serving Bellarmine College, Berea College, Centre
College of Kentucky, Eastern Kentucky University,
The Filson Club, Georgetown College, Kentucky
Historical Society, Kentucky State University,
Morehead State University, Murray State University,
Northern Kentucky University, Transylvania University,
University of Kentucky, University of Louisville,
and Western Kentucky University.

Editorial and Sales Offices: The University Press of Kentucky
663 South Limestone Street, Lexington, Kentucky 40508-4008

01 00 99 98 97   5 4 3 2 1

Library of Congress Cataloging-in-Publication Data
Rock art of Kentucky / Fred E. Coy, Jr. . . . [et al.].
    p.   cm. — (Perspectives on Kentucky's past)
    Includes bibliographical references and index.
    ISBN 0-8131-1986-3 (alk. paper)
    1. Indians of North America — Kentucky — Antiquities.
2. Petroglyphs — Kentucky. 3. Rock paintings — Kentucky.
4. Kentucky — Antiquities. I. Coy, Fred E., 1923-   . II. Series.
E78.K3R55   1996
976.9'01 — dc20   96-20466

CONTENTS

The Kentucky Heritage Council, the State Historic Preservation Office, is proud to sponsor this publication on the prehistoric petroglyphs and pictographs of Kentucky. An important part of our mission as a state agency is to locate, describe, evaluate, and protect historic and archaeological resources so they can be enjoyed by all Kentuckians. Our mission also includes disseminating information on Kentucky history and its prehistory to the public. To meet this need, the Council is sponsoring a series of books on the state's cultural resources. This volume is the fourth book in that series and the second dealing with archaeological sites.

For more than 12,000 years, Kentucky was the home of Native American peoples. All parts of the state were inhabited, some areas more intensely than others. Native Americans left behind many indications of their presence-- mounds, earthworks, and the archaeological remains of camps, villages, and workshop areas. At these sites can be found stone and bone tools and shards of their fired clay pottery. But there is one prehistoric site type, in particular, that often sparks public interest: stone carvings (petroglyphs) and paintings (pictographs), collectively referred to as rock art.

This overview of Kentucky's prehistoric rock art represents the culmination of more than thirty years of research by Dr. Fred Coy and Mr. Thomas Fuller of Louisville, Kentucky, and Mr. Larry Meadows of Clay City, Kentucky. These individuals have traveled throughout the state, searching for and documenting rock art sites. Too often during their visits, they discovered that many of the rock art sites had been altered or destroyed by vandals or sometimes stolen. In many cases the records prepared by Coy, Fuller, and Meadows are the only information that exists for sites that are now destroyed. With the additional assistance of Dr. Jim Swauger of the Carnegie Museum of Natural History, this record has been translated into a professional database, available to scholars throughout the nation.

As Director of the Kentucky Heritage Council, I want to recognize and congratulate Dr. Fred Coy, Mr. Tom Fuller, and Mr. Larry Meadows for their years of dedicated research into Kentucky's prehistoric rock art. The original investigations that form the core of this volume were conducted without public assistance and have provided the authors with no personal profit or gain, other than the satisfaction of having provided to the Commonwealth a service that cannot be repaid. The Kentucky Heritage Council feels privileged to have participated in this project. It has been a very rewarding experience for the Council's staff to work with the authors over the years and to see this book become a reality.

David L. Morgan, *Executive Director*

KENTUCKY HERITAGE COUNCIL
AND STATE HISTORIC PRESERVATION OFFICER

A chance discovery in May 1962 sparked an interest in Kentucky rock art that led to this book. Fred Coy and Tom Fuller, accompanied by Letcher Langston and Ernest Ellison, were on an early spring outing on the north fork of Rough River. While some of us were photographing wildflowers, one member of the group found a boulder with numerous bird tracks, a human handprint, and a mortar hole underneath an overhanging sandstone ledge near the river. These were obviously aboriginal in nature and in the discussion that followed, Tom Fuller mentioned the fact that he had seen two similar sites some years before, in Breckinridge and Meade Counties. Curiosity aroused, Coy and Fuller began looking for more information in local libraries and found that very little had been written on petroglyphs and pictographs in eastern United States.

During the next few months, they sent letters to various professional archaeologists working in the southeastern United States. In general, the letters were unanswered or the recipients knew nothing of petroglyphs. Meanwhile, Coy and Fuller visited several other petroglyph sites and began compiling a bibliography with the thought of writing papers on this subject. They authored several site reports over the next few years, and this book relies heavily on those discussions.

In early May 1969, Coy and Fuller met with James L. Swauger, then associate director of the Carnegie Museum in Pittsburgh and an authority on petroglyphs in Pennsylvania and Ohio. This began a collaboration that ultimately led to this publication. Larry Meadows joined the team in the spring of 1971 and offered his special knowledge of sites in the Cumberland Plateau of eastern Kentucky. As information on petroglyph sites in Kentucky grew, the idea of producing a book-length descriptive catalogue of the sites emerged. Following discussions between the Kentucky Heritage Council and the quartet of researchers, Mary Cronan Oppel, then director of the Kentucky Heritage Council and state historic preservation officer, based in Frankfort, requested that Swauger submit a survey and planning grant application to review the information assembled by Coy, Fuller, and Meadows and evaluate its suitability for publication. Swauger submitted an application dated 24 October 1983, in which he proposed a program of field and library study designed to test the records of his three colleagues. Approved in April 1984, the project was conducted under Grant No. 21-84-8107.

By December 1985, preliminary field work had been completed and all funds were expended or committed. The information reviewed by Swauger clearly supported the evaluation that a volume on petroglyphs would be a useful addition to the literature on the archaeology of Kentucky. In 1986, David L. Morgan, who had succeeded Mrs. Oppel as director of the Kentucky Heritage Council, issued a letter of agreement addressed to Swauger to fund the preparation of a manuscript on Kentucky rock art. Swauger took the information collected by Coy, Fuller, Meadows, and himself and produced a draft manuscript that forms the basis of this book. It was implicit in the understanding between the contributors and the council that while formal agreements and notifications were to be addressed to Swauger, and while he would be doing the bulk of the assembling of information for presentation in book form, the authors of the work would be Coy, Fuller, Meadows, and Swauger, in that order, and that all shared responsibility for accumulation of data and accuracy of presentation. The first draft of the manuscript was completed and submitted to the Kentucky Heritage Council in 1987. As new data became available, revisions of the manuscript continued through 1995.

Since submission of the initial draft manuscript, a thematic nomination of eligible petroglyph sites was compiled by Jimmy Railey (then a staff member of the Kentucky Heritage Council) in order to be listed on the National Register of Historic Places. The nomination was favorably reviewed at all levels and the sites were officially listed on the National Register on 8 September 1989.

Certain questions might be asked about this study: Why this book? Why now? Why these authors? The answers, especially to the last, involve a consideration of the history of the subject. Until recently, recording the marks left on stone by Native Americans has fallen to persons untrained in archaeology. The first such records in Eastern United States were made by members of the clergy. The earliest was a 1673 description of a pictograph in what is now western Illinois by explorer and Catholic priest Jacques Marquette. In 1680, John Danforth, a New England minister, made notes on a petroglyph in Massachusetts, and his report was published by another noted New England clergyman, Cotton Mather, in 1690. Henry Roe Schoolcraft, trained as a chemist and glass maker, became active in the Bureau of Indian Affairs in the mid-1800s and published many accounts of the "pictographic writings" of the American Indian.

The first comprehensive account of the "picture writing" of the Native American was produced by attorney Garrick Mallery while at the Bureau of Ethnology in the late nineteenth century. In 1967, Campbell Grant, a California artist, was the first to present the subject as "rock art" in a book for a popular audience. That work was followed in 1979 by a scholarly treatise on North American rock art by Klaus Wellmann, a New York pathologist.

We are now at a transitional point in the study of these marks left on the rocks for us to ponder. Until now the theme has been, of necessity, seek, record, and protect. Now it is time for the old school—present authors included—to turn to the professional archaeologist to advance this study through the use of state-of-the-art scientific tools.

What we present in this book are the fruits of our seeking and recording. While volumes have been published on petroglyphs and pictographs in the West and Northeast, this is the first book to describe rock art in Southeastern United States. We present this information in a form that we hope will be interesting and educational for the public. We would like to create an awareness of the value of preserving these fragile contacts with our prehistoric, preliterate Kentuckians. It is also our hope that the professional archaeologist will find this a useful starting point for further investigations.

When a data collection project spans many years and includes many sites, it is inevitable that one becomes indebted to many people for help and information. The contributors to this volume were helped by many individuals who provided comparative information from other states or countries as well as local residents of many Kentucky counties who told us of sites and often arranged for us to visit them. Professional archaeologists such as Alfred K. Guthe and Charles Faulkner (University of Tennessee), Martha Ann Rolingson, Lathel Duffield, Michael Collins, and John Dorwin (all formerly with the University of Kentucky), Patty Jo Watson and Carol Diaz-Granádos (Washington University), and geologists Garland Dever (Kentucky Geological Survey) and Benjamin Gildersleeve (U.S. Geological Survey) all contributed their knowledge and expertise at various times. We also received help from Pat Vinnicombe of South Africa and Lila Fundaburk and Klaus F. Wellmann of New York City. A conference organized by Jim Swauger in 1975 at Powder Mill near Pittsburgh enabled us to meet other researchers interested in rock art and learn more about their findings.

During the past several years Cecil Ison, Daniel Boone National Forest archaeologist, and Tom Fouts, zone archaeologist with the Daniel Boone National Forest, have supplied their professional expertise in the locating and recording of several new sites. They have been instrumental in initiating a program with Dr. K. Lal Gauri, director of the Stone Conservation Laboratory at the University of Louisville, to evaluate the weather-related degradation of the Kentucky petroglyphs, and we hope they will be able to suggest methods of site preservation.

Several local Kentucky residents helped us many times over the years.

These include Grace Bandy of Cloverport for her many hours of work, both on the phone and on-site in her part of the state; Steve Bentley, who found several sites for us, did much research, and spent many days with us on field trips; and Johnny Faulkner, who accompanied us on field trips, helped carry equipment, acted as a guide, furnished transportation for Jim Swauger, and was helpful in other ways too numerous to mention. Glyn Rogers also helped on many of our field trips, pursued sites, and made contacts with local people. Chance acquaintances with Dewey Ward and Michael Flener led to petroglyph sites on Green River, and Blanche DeMunbrun was able to obtain permission from Guss Parsley on a pictograph site in Edmonson County. John Tierney of the Carter Caves State Park reviewed some of the early archaeological literature published by the University of Kentucky and helped us find pictographs in the Carter Caves area. Michael Hensley, of Oneida, Kentucky, and his family enabled us to visit several sites in Clay County. Don Fig of the U.S. Forest Service was most helpful to us for sites in the area around the Red River Gorge. We have relied heavily on Ernest Ellison for information regarding photographic techniques, and he also has visited many of our sites.

In addition, we would like to list various people who have helped us over the years: Don Alexander, Steve Ashley, Carliss Bentley, Jimmy Bentley, Randy Boedy, Betty Broyles, Raymond Carrol, Lee Casper, Lloyd M. Chapman, Tom Davis, David Deering, Mr. and Mrs. James R. Farris, Robert Frazier, Elman Fulks, Floyd Ginter, Roy and Morris Harrington, Ed Hayslette, Elmer Hensley, Eugene Hettiger, Bet Ison, Jack King, Dallas Knox, Charlie Long, Carl McIntosh, Homer Matthews, Faye Meadows, Lief Meadows, Donald Morton, Duwain Morton, Charles Perdue and sons, Thomas N. Sanders, Harry W. Scott, Bill Sharp, Dan Skidmore, Eddie Skinner, Bob Smith, Jerry Smith, Eli Sparks, Vernon Spratt, Jerry Steele, Roland A. Stephens, Dale and Darrell Stevens, Mrs. Everette Stevenson, Douglas Travis, Richard White, Jr., Vernon White, and Boyd Williams.

Nancy O'Malley had the unique ability to relate with the subject and the personalities of the authors and bring order out of chaos. It has been a pleasure to work with Mrs. O'Malley as she has done an excellent job editing this volume.

Without the resolve of David L. Morgan, executive director of the Kentucky Heritage Council, and the editorial skills of Julie Riesenweber, this book could never have become a reality. From the time the idea of the book was conceived, Charles Hockensmith, archaeologist with the Kentucky Heritage Council, has acted as a liaison between the authors and the council. He has shepherded us through both good times and bad without losing his composure.

We take our hat off to him. Charles Hockensmith has taken charge of the final editing, contacting the individuals for review of the manuscript, and has rewritten all of the site locations to make them general. The precise locations are on file with the Kentucky Heritage Council.

Perhaps the person to whom we are most indebted is Emily Coy, my dear wife. She has graciously entertained various visitors over the years, furnishing meals, both at home and on field trips. She never complains about the clutter of photographs, books, and papers. She is always willing to fill in as a research or field assistant, and she never complains about her husband's frequent weekend absences to visit new sites.

—Fred E. Coy, Jr.

1

INTRODUCTION

Archaeologists use the term "artifact" to describe the material remains of human activity by extinct cultures. Artifacts include such diverse items as stone tools, human skeletons, ceramic shards from cooking pots, animal bones discarded from meals, ornaments of bone, shell, and other natural materials, and engraved or painted symbols or drawings on boulders, rock outcrops, and the walls of caves, rockshelters, or cliffs.

These latter artifacts, called "petroglyphs" and "pictographs," are the subject of this book. Petroglyphs are designs engraved on rocks by carving, pecking, rubbing, or a combination of these methods. (See the glossary for more detailed definitions of terms.) Pictographs are designs painted on rocks.

Petroglyphs, pictographs, and works combining these techniques are generally described by the term "rock art." Some may argue that few if any of the designs carved or painted on rocks in Kentucky served as or were intended to be art by their makers, but the term is in general use and is employed in this work from time to time.

Rock art has fascinated professional researchers and laymen alike for hundreds of years. Despite many published descriptions of petroglyphs and pictographs from all over the world, the meaning behind the symbols and representations remains enigmatic in many cases. Before meaning can be analyzed, we must compile a comprehensive record of the location and physical characteristics of rock art sites and of the design elements and motifs represented in them. It is the fundamental purpose of this book to provide a comprehensive descriptive catalog of rock art sites in Kentucky so that the necessary information for analysis is available.

We embarked on this study with several assumptions that guided our work. An important element is our belief that the "what, where, and how" must be known before the "when, who, and why" can be deduced. Our research documented many different design elements and motifs, some occurring in isolation and some forming repeated patterns.

If a design is often repeated, we feel justified in suggesting that it had meaning for the cultural groups to which the carvers belonged. The repetition might just as well signify, however, only that it was a design easily engraved or particularly pleasing to the carvers. We further hypothesize that groups of designs composing discrete patterns may each be associated with other variables such as characteristics of site location. If such correlations exist, commonly understood meaning was surely present among the cultural groups producing the designs. If relationships between rock art and Native American groups can be confirmed, we may be able to offer explanations of the purpose of the designs and patterns, and of the sites individually and as components of groups of sites. Similar analysis has been attempted for designs on Tlingit halibut hooks, relating them to Tlingit culture as a whole (Jonaitis 1981).

Despite this brave exposition of theory, we must confess that while we know where Native American rock art sites are in Kentucky, know what their contents are, know how they were made, and can make reasonable guesses as to when they were created, we do not yet know who carved and painted them or why. We have yet to find a meaningful matrix of designs or patterns of designs that can lead us to who and why, and we are left only with the hope that some day we will find such a matrix.

As we and others working east of the Mississippi River continue to amass, organize, and ponder data, the matrix may emerge, for this great reach of habitat is a large and relatively homogeneous archaeological and ethnological region (Caldwell 1958, viii; Kroeber 1963, 60; Stoltman 1978, 706, 711–12), and some day the touchstone may be found.

The geology of Kentucky is dominated by sedimentary rocks with formations of the Pennsylvanian and Mississippian Ages being found on the surface in both eastern and western Kentucky. The older formations in central Kentucky are near the center of a large geologic bubble known as the Cincinnati Arch. This arch was lifted during the Paleozoic Era and the younger rocks eroded from the surface, exposing in successive layers older sedimentary rocks. Pennsylvanian and Mississippian rocks are composed of shale, silt-stone, sandstone, limestone, and coal members. Limestones primarily weath-er by dissolution, leaving smoother surfaces than do the sandstones, which tend to fragment and form large cliffs. In some areas, erosion of massive sand-stone members formed the so-called rock houses or rockshelters in which pet-roglyphs and pictographs are preserved.

The Cincinnati Arch in central Kentucky and the weathering of lime-stones are responsible for the outcropping of Ordovician Age rocks, the oldest in the state. Younger formations are distributed in successive layers extend-ing from the center of the Cincinnati Arch near Lexington in the Bluegrass region. Their distributional order is Silurian, Devonian, Pennsylvanian, and Mississippian. It is in these latter rocks that a series of escarpments are found extending from the Ohio River in Mason County to the Tennessee border in central Kentucky and then back to the Ohio River in Meade and Breckinridge Counties. Streams that flow into this escarpment from the surrounding Penn-sylvanian and Mississippian formations tend to make deep channels through the sandstone, leaving massive cliffs. Typical examples occur in the Red River Gorge area of eastern Kentucky and, to a lesser degree, in western Kentucky. All along these cliffs are found rockshelters that frequently show evidence of prehistoric human habitation. Sandstone boulders on the floor and the walls of these rockshelters are quite friable when freshly exposed, but weathering causes a durable "crust" or cortex to be formed on the surface. Designs are eas-ily engraved on freshly fractured sandstone, but once the surface forms a cor-tex, it becomes much less friable. This weathering process occurs fairly rapid-ly, making modern carvings difficult to distinguish from prehistoric carvings. All of the petroglyphs in Kentucky are engraved on sandstone except a ques-tionable example on a Meade County limestone cliff and a pictograph painted on a limestone formation in Carter County.

In 1974, Swauger published his methodology for documenting petroglyphs and pictographs. He listed twelve specific steps used where possible to record a site and its contents (Swauger 1974, 24–27). In his study of the rock art of Ohio, he did not religiously follow the methods applied to the work reported in 1974, although he utilized most of them (Swauger 1984, 2–4). He was able to perform in this fashion because it was his work alone, conducted according to his planned program.

The information on which this work is based was not accumulated as the result of a specific research program conducted by one person with the even-tual goal of a published volume. Rather, this study is the result of research begun in 1964, and it was not until 1986 that the writing of a book-length report on the petroglyphs and pictographs of Kentucky was commissioned.

The data were accumulated over a period of thirty-two years under widely varying conditions and by the coauthors working both individually and together. This research situation was not designed to result in a comprehensive volume but rather the kind of specific site reports listed in the bibliography under the joint authorship of Coy and Fuller. Because of this lack of a specific goal, and because of constraints of time and resources, particularly from April 1984 through June 1987, lengthy investigations like those presented in Swauger's 1974 and 1984 volumes were not possible. As a result, our reporting of the sites is on occasion uneven. For this no apologies are made. We endeavored to insure that the basic recording was reasonably complete, doing the best we could with the resources and time available. We believe we here provide essential information on which future studies of these phenomena can be based to reach fuller understanding and perhaps explanations for the petroglyphs and pictographs of Kentucky.

Bearing in mind the above caveat, we did in general pursue a standard recording system. We documented physical contexts (sites) in which petroglyphs and pictographs occur by both written description and photographs (including black and white prints as well as color slides) and video tapes of many of the sites. We mapped the local geography of the sites and recorded their specific locations. We recorded the cardinal directions of the rockshelters' openings. We drew sketch maps of petroglyphs and pictographs and of the rocks on which they occur. We incorporated a means of determining scale in our photographs or sketches and/or recorded linear dimensions in our sketches and in our written descriptions. We made preliminary lists of designs using general terms, when we could, as guides for future evaluation and as records of our initial reactions. Initially, Coy and Fuller (1966, 54) made latex molds and plaster casts of the petroglyphs. Cost and fear of damaging the petroglyph precluded such recording in later years. It is to be remembered that before 1986 public funds were not available to defray costs. Coy, Fuller, and Meadows paid their own expenses throughout the duration of the study.

Early in his studies of petroglyphs, Swauger used chalk to emphasize the lines of designs (Swauger 1961, 106–12). Chalking is now a widely condemned procedure (Lee 1991, 13). On occasion during his work in Kentucky, Swauger used salt to bring out the lines of petroglyphs in dim light. Johnny Faulkner modified this approach by sprinkling dirt from a rockshelter floor in the grooves of a design. Coy and Fuller argued that such attempts were inappropriate because elements can be added or deleted during the application.

Swauger was in general agreement with these sentiments; nevertheless, he periodically used one or another of these techniques, and he alone is responsible for all such cases.

The best known, most widely used site names were used to identify the sites. In cases where a site was known by more than one name, we used the most widely recognized one. Temporary field numbers were assigned to each site during survey. Each site was later assigned a permanent trinomial designation issued by the Office of State Archaeology (OSA). The OSA site designation eliminates confusion likely to be caused by the use of names only. In his 1974 and 1984 works, Swauger numbered and named each design in his study sites. Except for a few cases—such as the Wickliffe Site (15BA109), where designs were known from literature, and the Ashley Site (15ES27)—designs of most of the sites were not numbered. We hope our descriptions and illustrations are sufficient for the reader to identify and understand the designs documented at the sites.

Distance and elevation records in this work were normally measured on United States Geological Survey topographic quadrangles. Unless otherwise noted, all quadrangles used were of the 7.5-Minute Series of the United States Geological Survey. Specific directions to the sites are eliminated from this publication because such preciseness often leads to site destruction by vandals. Those who wish to know exact site locations should apply to the Kentucky Heritage Council, where such records exist. Council representatives can then decide the legitimacy of each request and act accordingly.

We studied and recorded many reported sites even when some sites proved or were believed to be Euro-American, natural, or forged. Swauger (1960, 64) wrote that he studied, recorded, and reported both natural and Euro-American sites so that "a responsible journal might bear witness that an investigation of this site has been conducted." In this work on the rock art of Kentucky, we pursue the same approach. Each of the Kentucky sites was assigned to one of four categories: Native American origin, Euro-American origin, Natural origin, and Uncertain origin. These judgments were collectively made on the basis of our cumulative observation and knowledge and the expertise of other workers whom we consulted.

The rock art data gathered during this project are housed in several centers. Chief of these is the State Historic Preservation Office of the Kentucky Heritage Council, Frankfort, where the central, formal record is filed. It is to this source that interested persons should first apply for information.

What amounts to a duplicate set of records that apply specifically to this study is a "voucher" set held at the Division of Anthropology, Carnegie Museum, Pittsburgh. The division's holdings and those of the Historic Preservation Office have more information in the form of reports, maps, photographs, and other sorts of data than are specifically mentioned or used in this volume.

In the Carnegie files, each site is separately filed in a folder containing correspondence, black-and-white and color prints, overlays of locations based on topographic sheets and site plans, bibliographical information, copies of published information, drawings of designs, and other sorts of records.

Black-and-white and color negatives, prints, and transparencies of sites and designs are numbered and cataloged in files of both the Carnegie Museum and Swauger. Bibliographical records are also maintained at Carnegie.

In harmony with the policy of Carnegie Museum to be of as much service as possible to interested persons, the records on the petroglyph work are available for study in the museum by qualified individuals upon application and scheduling.

Coy, Fuller, and Meadows each have their own photographic and other records. None, to date, has shown any reluctance to share them with other interested persons trying to know and understand rock art phenomena.

Sixty-two rock art sites with petroglyphs or pictographs in nineteen counties were classified as being of Native American manufacture. They are listed in Table 1 and discussed in Chapter 2. Nine sites in eight counties either were destroyed before they could be examined by the authors or were of questionable origin and, for various reasons, could not be located for evaluation. These are listed in Table 2 and discussed in Chapter 3. Early in the course of compiling information on petroglyph sites, the Office of State Archaeology assigned permanent numbers to sites for which locations could be determined, even if a site no longer existed. Site numbers were not assigned where precise locations could not be determined from available references.

TABLE 1

Native American Petroglyph and Pictograph Sites in Kentucky

Site Name	County	Permanent Site Number	Field Site Number
Mattingly	Breckinridge	15BC128	CMNH-15BC1
Tar Springs	Breckinridge	15BC129	CMNH-15BC2
North Fork of Rough River	Breckinridge	15BC130	CMNH-15BC3
Baby Track Rock	Butler	15BT40	CMNH-15BT2
Turkey Rock	Butler	15BT64	CMNH-15BT1
Reedyville	Butler	15BT65	CMNH-15BT3
Carter Caves	Carter	15CR60	CMNH-15CR1
Pilot Rock	Christian	15CH200	CMNH-15CH200
Bar Creek	Clay	15CY18	CMNH-15CY4
Red Bird River	Clay	15CY51	CMNH-15CY1
Red Bird River Shelter	Clay	15CY52	CMNH-15CY2
Fish Trap Rock	Clay	15CY53	CMNH-15CY3
Laurel Branch	Clay	15CY265	none
Dismal Rock	Edmonson	15ED15	CMNH-15ED2
Asphalt Rock Pictographs	Edmonson	15ED24	CMNH-15ED1
Little Fairdale	Edmonson	15ED96	CMNH-15ED3
Big Gimlet	Elliott	15EL3	CMNH-15EL1
Sparks Indian Rock House	Estill	15ES26	CMNH-15ES1
Ashley	Estill	15ES27	CMNH-15ES2
Sparks II	Estill	15ES59	none
Crow Hollow	Grayson	15GY65	CMNH-15GY3
Saltsman Branch	Grayson	15GY66	CMNH-15GY1
Saltsman Branch Shelter	Grayson	15GY67	CMNH-15GY2
Jeffry Cliff	Hancock	15HA114	CMNH-15HA1
Daugherty Bear Track	Jackson	15JA160	CMNH-15JA1
Brushy Ridge	Jackson	15JA161	CMNH-15JA3
William Gay	Jackson	15JA234	none

continued

TABLE 1

continued

Site Name	County	Permanent Site Number	Field Site Number
Christmas Eve	Jackson	15JA235	CMNH-15JA4
Peter Cave Branch	Jackson	15JA355	none
Big Turtle Shelter	Lee	15LE55	none
Big Sinking Creek Turtle Rock	Lee	15LE57	CMNH-15LE2
Cave Fork Hill	Lee	15LE110	CMNH-15LE5
Perdue	Lee	15LE111	CMNH-15LE3
Bear Track	Lee	15LE112	CMNH-15LE1
Old Landing	Lee	15LE113	CMNH-15LE6
Fincastle	Lee	15LE120	CMNH-15LE4
Little Sinking	Lee	15LE215	none
Mantle Rock	Livingston	15LV160	none
Burnt Ridge	Madison	15MA197	CMNH-15MA1
Payneville	Meade	15MD308	CMNH-15MD2
Indian Stairway	Menifee	15MF160	CMNH-15MF2
Stone Foot Shelter	Menifee	15MF178	none
Bell's Falls	Menifee	15MF199	CMNH-15MF4
Spratt's	Menifee	15MF353	CMNH-15MF5
Skidmore	Menifee	15MF354	CMNH-15MF1
Martin Fork	Powell	15PO23	CMNH-15PO1
High Rock	Powell	15PO25	CMNH-15PO3
State Rock	Powell	15PO106	CMNH-15PO7
McKinney Bluff	Powell	15PO107	CMNH-15PO9
Amburgy Hollow	Powell	15PO108	CMNH-15PO2
White's	Powell	15PO154	CMNH-15PO4
Nada Tunnel 1	Powell	15PO155	CMNH-15PO5
Nada Tunnel 2	Powell	15PO156	CMNH-15PO6
Branham Ridge	Powell	15PO158	CMNH-15PO10
Knox	Powell	15PO159	CMNH-15PO12
Steven DeHart	Powell	15PO160	CMNH-15PO11

continued

TABLE 1

continued

Site Name	County	Permanent Site Number	Field Site Number
Ledford Hollow	Powell	15PO281	none
Loman Hill	Rockcastle	15RK49	CMNH-15RK1
Jabez	Russell	15RU42	CMNH-15RU1
Caesar Hurst Shelter	Wolfe	15WO19	CMNH-15WO3
Trinity Shelter	Wolfe	15WO26	CMNH-15WO2
Seventeen Seventeen	Wolfe	15WO119	none

TABLE 2

Destroyed or Questionable Petroglyph and Pictograph Sites in Kentucky

Site Name	County	Permanent Site Number	Field Site Number
Wickliffe	Ballard	15BA109	CMNH-15BA1
Catlettsburg	Boyd	15BD81	CMNH-15BD1
Portsmouth Indian Head	Greenup	15GP173	CMNH-15GP1
Grayson Springs	Grayson	none	CMNH-15GY4
Pine Knob	Grayson	15GY68	CMNH-15GY5
Clover Bottom	Jackson	15JA162	CMNH-15JA2
Little Mud Creek Pictograph	Johnson	15JO3	CMNH-15JO1
Unnamed	Lewis	15LW93	CMNH-15LW1
Unnamed	Union	none	CMNH-15UN2

2

NATIVE AMERICAN SITES

MATTINGLY PETROGLYPH SITE (15BC128)

LOCATION: Breckinridge County, north of Mattingly and south of Cloverport, on the Mattingly Quadrangle, in a rockshelter in a small valley near the western bank of Caney Creek; the rockshelter faces generally to the north, where a small, wet-weather stream joins the creek (Coy and Fuller 1966, 54). Elevation: 160 m (520 ft).

DESCRIPTION: The rockshelter measures 6 m (20 ft) in width, 2.5 m (8 ft) in height and 2.5 m (8 ft) in depth (Fig. 1) and is open on three sides. A large rock measuring 6 m (20 ft) in length, 2 m (6.5 ft) in width and 1 m (3 ft 10 in) in height has fallen from the shelter roof. The face of this rock is angled at a slope of 30 degrees. The petroglyphs were carved upon this rock face and include 63 bird tracks, 3 deer tracks, and 3 sets of rabbit tracks (Figs. 2, 3). One set of pit-and-groove designs were also documented. On the top central portion of the rock is a large hominy hole, measuring 61 cm (2 ft) in depth and 12 cm (4.75 in) in diameter at its opening (Coy and Fuller 1966, 54).

This site is typical of the sandstone rockshelters in which petroglyphs occur in the Pennyroyal Region of northcentral Kentucky. Coy and Fuller

1. View of the Mattingly rockshelter. The petroglyphs are on the inner facing portion of the boulder in the front of the rockshelter. Klaus Wellmann (1979), noted rock art authority, and his wife, Margot, are pictured.

(1966, 53) noted the frequent presence of "hominy holes" in ledges at the rockshelter entrances. The ledges also occasionally contained petroglyphs, frequently depicting distinctly incised animal tracks of various kinds and human hand- and footprints.

BIBLIOGRAPHIC SOURCES: Coy and Fuller 1966; Fuller 1969a.

FIRST RECORDED BY AUTHORS: Coy and Fuller, April 1963.

2. The Mattingly petroglyphs.

3. Drawing of the Mattingly petroglyphs

TAR SPRINGS PETROGLYPH SITE (15BC129)

LOCATION: Breckinridge County; designs carved on a sandstone block in a rockshelter on the Mattingly Quadrangle; near Tar Springs and the Mattingly Site (15BC128). Elevation: 170 m (560 ft).

DESCRIPTION: The rockshelter faces south and measures 9.75 m (32 ft) in depth and 18 m (60 ft) in height (Fig. 4). The petroglyphs were described by Coy and Fuller (1968, 29–30):

> The engravings are carved on the inner face of a free standing sandstone block, 4' to 6' [1.2–1.8 m] high, 6 1/2' [1.6 m] long and 4' [1.2 m] wide. The face is slanted with the horizontal 24° with the lower edge toward the back of the rockshelter. From the outer face of the block a slab 5' [.9 m] long, 3' [1.5 m] high and 1 1/2' [.5 m] wide has fallen forward. The surface of the slab which

4. View of the Tar Springs rockshelter showing the large sandstone slab bearing petroglyphs.

was continuous with the upper surface of the block, also contains engravings. When the slab fell forward, it became imbedded in the floor of the rockshelter and has sustained more damage from weathering than the protected face of the block. . . .

Designs are pecked into the surface of the block and generally are quite easily identified. There are several areas on which the pecking can be seen however without recognizable designs.

There are 12 circular carvings, 17 bird tracks, several indefinite linear designs, and as stated above, other designs that cannot be recognized. On the slab that had fallen from the block at the point of the fracture is a hole 2" [5 cm] in diameter by 3" [7.5 cm] deep which is surrounded by a circle. This does not have the smoothness nor the size of the so-called "hominy holes." There is a "hominy hole," however, in a nearby boulder 4" [10 cm] in diameter and 11" [27.5 cm] deep. The largest complete design is a spiral 10" [25 cm] in diameter that terminates at the center in a shallow circular depression.

Figures 5 and 6 illustrate the petroglyphs. They include:
   1. large clockwise spiral (partial double helix);
   2. circle and pit;
   3. concentric circles with a geometric projection;
   4. one bird track;
   5. two examples of circle-and-pit elements separated by pecking marks;
   6. circle and straight line;
   7. indefinite circular motif;
   8. circle with pits above bird track (incomplete or obscured designs to the right);
   9. circular motif;
   10. linear motif enclosing no. 6;
   11. cluster of bird tracks;
   12. deer track and circle and pit;
   13. small cluster of bird tracks;
   14. indefinite curvilinear design;
   15. indefinite designs or peck marks.

Coy and Fuller (1966, 30) noted that the Tar Springs petroglyphs were in close proximity to the Mattingly petroglyphs and shared some similarities. Both shelters contained bird tracks and a hominy hole. Circles and spirals were unique to the Tar Springs site. Unlike designs elsewhere, which were produced by a combination of pecking and grinding, these petroglyphs were produced by percussion methods.

BIBLIOGRAPHIC SOURCES: Coy and Fuller 1968; Fuller 1969a.

FIRST RECORDED BY AUTHORS: Coy and Fuller, October 1967.

5. Sandstone slab bearing the Tar Springs petroglyphs.

6. Composite drawing of petroglyphs in the Tar Springs rockshelter.

NORTH FORK OF ROUGH RIVER PETROGLYPH SITE (15BC130)

LOCATION: Breckinridge County, east of St. Anthony's School and south of Roff on the Kingswood Quadrangle; Coy and Fuller (1966, 54) described the location as being "on the North Fork of the Rough River . . . in the sharp bend of the river . . . on the north bank. . . . It is within the U.S. Reservation boundary for the Rough River Reservoir." Elevation: 170 m (550 ft).

DESCRIPTION: The petroglyphs are within a relatively large, south-facing rockshelter, measuring 27.5 m (90 ft) in width, 5.8 m (19 ft) in depth and 4 m (13 ft) in height (Fig. 7). A piece of sandstone roof fall measuring 2.6 m (8.75 ft) in length, 1.2 m (3.8 ft) in width, and 0.9 m (3 ft) in height lies well within the rockshelter. Its upper surface has at least 14 bird tracks and a human hand print as well as two small hominy holes (Fig. 8). One hole is considerably deeper than the other (Coy and Fuller 1966, 54).

BIBLIOGRAPHIC SOURCES: Coy and Fuller 1966.

FIRST RECORDED BY AUTHORS: Coy and Fuller, March 1962.

7. View of the North Fork of Rough River rockshelter.

8. Petroglyphs in the North Fork of Rough River rockshelter.

BABY TRACK ROCK PETROGLYPH SITE (15BT40)

LOCATION: Butler County, in a sandstone rockshelter near the head of a valley overlooking Welch's Creek; it is north-northwest of Mount Union Church and west-northwest of Cedar Grove School on the Riverside Quadrangle; Coy and Fuller (1966, 54) described its location as "3 miles north of the junction of the Green and Barren Rivers . . . on the north end of a ridge locally known as the 'hogback ridge'." Elevation: about 180 m (600 ft).

DESCRIPTION: Coy and Fuller (1966, 54–55) described this sandstone rockshelter as measuring 13.2 m (44 ft) in width, 3 m (10 ft) in height, and 3 m (10 ft) in depth (Fig. 9). The petroglyphs were inscribed on a large section of roof fall. They consist of five human footprints varying in size from 5 by 7.5 cm (2 by 3 in) to 10 by 25 cm (4 by 10 in) (Figs. 10, 11). The petroglyphs are carved in the face of a rock with a slope exceeding 45 degrees. The horizontal face of the rock above these representations contains three well-formed but shallow hominy holes. Coy and Fuller (1966, 54–55) were told that a sixth footprint larger than any of the rest was buried beneath a relic collector's backdirt pile.

The rockshelter containing the petroglyphs was documented by Kentucky Heritage Council archaeologist Charles Hockensmith during May of 1981. Artifacts collected from looters' backdirt piles included thin limestone tempered ceramic shards, an expanded stem projectile point, bifaces, chert flakes, bone fragments, and mussel shell fragments (Hockensmith 1981). The ceramics and the projectile point suggest that Late Woodland people lived in the rockshelter. However, the petroglyphs are not in direct association with the Late Woodland artifacts. It is also possible that other prehistoric peoples utilizing the site produced the petroglyphs before and after the Late Woodland occupation.

BIBLIOGRAPHIC SOURCES: Coy and Fuller 1966; Hockensmith 1981.

FIRST RECORDED BY AUTHORS: Coy and Fuller, November 1965.

9. View of the Baby Track rockshelter.

10. Footprints in the Baby Track rockshelter.

11. Drawing of footprints in the Baby Track rockshelter.

TURKEY ROCK PETROGLYPH SITE (15BT64)

LOCATION: Butler County, on the banks of, and sometimes is flooded by, the Green River; it is north of Allens Hill on the Morgantown Quadrangle. Coy and Fuller (1967, 58) described it as being "at the upper arm of an 'S' shaped curve of Green River known as Big Bend . . . between miles 140 and 141."

DESCRIPTION: The petroglyphs were carved on a projection of sandstone, facing upstream (southeast) and extending into Green River from the southwest bank (Fig. 12). The rock is frequently flooded; when exposed it is usually obscured by a thick layer of tenacious mud (Coy and Fuller 1967, 58–59). The carvings cover an area measuring 1.5 m (4 ft) by 3.2 m (10.6 ft). The rock face lies at an angle of 30 degrees.

The carvings consist of enclosed quadrangles, tracks, punctate designs, and linear elements incised into the surface with lines measuring 1.25–3.75 cm (.5–1.5 in) in width and 0.3 cm (0.13 in) in depth (Figs. 13–15). The lines are rather irregular, suggesting that they may well have been incised by percussion rather than by abrasion.

12. View of the Turkey Rock petroglyph site.

13. Composite drawing of Turkey Rock petroglyphs.

14. Unique example of a quadrangular motif at Turkey Rock.

15. Example of a quadrangular motif with
wavy lines at Turkey Rock.

Six quadrangular figures vary in size from 30 cm (12 in) to 15 cm (6 in) on
each side (Fig. 13). A unique example has double lines with rounded corners
on three sides and a third line between the double lines on one side (Fig. 14).
Several rows of 1.5 cm (0.5 in) punctates lie within the perimeter of the double lines. The remaining five quadrangular motifs contain a series of irregular, undulating lines (Fig. 15). At least 11 bird tracks, measuring 8 cm (3 in) in
length, are scattered among the quadrangular designs. Less definite animal
tracks are distributed across the upper section of the design group.

Four punctate groupings are scattered around the designs. They consist of
four to six 1.25 cm (0.5 in) dots arranged in circles measuring 7.5–10 cm (3–4
in) in diameter. Other miscellaneous petroglyphs include a triangular carving
and an irregular serpentine line with three large oval punctates.

The Turkey Rock petroglyphs are well preserved and show few signs of
defacement. Their state of preservation is due to (1) the oblique angle of the
rock face on which they are carved, (2) the denseness of the sandstone, (3)

their isolated location, only easily reached by boat, (4) their frequent submergence underwater, and (5) the protective mud layer that frequently covers them. A modern carving consisting of the initials "G. W. '32" and two tobacco pipes occur on the upper surface of the rock.

Despite frequent exploration and archaeological research in this portion of the Green River, these carvings have not been previously described. Moore's 1916 steamboat expedition up the Green River must have passed by—or above—the rock late in December 1915 or early in January 1916. According to U.S. Army Corps of Engineers records of November 1915 through February 1916, the rock was under water much of that time.

Coy and Fuller were taken to the site by an older resident of the county who saw the petroglyphs while swimming there in his youth. During one of the visits by the authors, an old fisherman/trapper stopped and stated he had passed this point many times and had not noticed them.

Interest in petroglyphs in the Big Bend area also seems low because they are not found in association with datable artifacts. These carvings were recorded by use of color transparencies, black-and-white photography, and by molds using CMC cold casting compounds. Molds of some of the figures have been made, but high water levels prevented complete documentation. Prior to the construction of the lock and dam system on the Green River, the water flow was very slow on some occasions. The petroglyphs may have formerly been much more visible than at present.

BIBLIOGRAPHIC SOURCES: Coy and Fuller 1967; Fuller 1969a, 1969b; Moore 1916.

FIRST RECORDED BY AUTHORS: Coy and Fuller, October 1966.

REEDYVILLE PETROGLYPH SITE (15BT65)

LOCATION: Butler County, southeast of Reedyville on the Reedyville Quadrangle. Coy and Fuller (1966) placed this site in the southeastern corner of the county near the old Honaker's Ferry. It is on the north side of a bend of the Green River north and west of the river. Elevation about 150 m (500 ft).

DESCRIPTION: The carvings are on an outcropping of lower Pennsylvanian sandstone locally known as the Caseyville Formation (Shaw 1966), which runs along the western bank of a small creek (Fig. 16). About 90 m (300 ft) below the site, the creek falls rather precipitously over a cliff near the Green River

16. View of the Reedyville petroglyph site (Tom Fuller and Pat Vinnicombe pictured).

floodplain. The surface on which the petroglyphs appear is roughly triangular and measures 7.5 m (24.5 ft) along its base, 2.8 m (9.25 ft) in height, and 9 m (30 ft) on the remaining side. The rock faces northeast.

The figures on the rock consist of several tracks, including at least five bird tracks, four human footprints, and an arm-and-hand print, pit-and-groove elements, and circles (Figs. 17, 18). Pecking, abrasion, and incision were used to produce the designs. Several circles have three or more pits within their circumference, and one has a cross (Fig. 19). One area of the rock exhibits four pits arranged in a square with a fifth pit in the center. The life-sized hand and arm have a line incised across the hand with a circle enclosing three pits at one end of the line. The predominant figure on the rock is that of a person with both arms outstretched above the head and standing on a circle that is transected vertically with a line to the foot.

The Reedyville Site occurs within 15 miles of one pictograph and five petroglyph sites (Coy and Fuller 1966, 1967, 1968, and 1969a; Fuller 1969a and 1969b). The six sites we have found in this area are very near Green River or are a short distance from the river on one of its tributaries. The Reedyville site bird track design is similar to those at four of the nearby sites. Human footprints have been documented at thirteen other sites. The profiled human figure at Reedyville has not been found elsewhere. A bedrock mortar is found in a rockshelter a few meters south of the exposed petroglyph rock.

BIBLIOGRAPHIC SOURCES: Coy and Fuller 1970.

FIRST RECORDED BY AUTHORS: Coy and Fuller, October 1969.

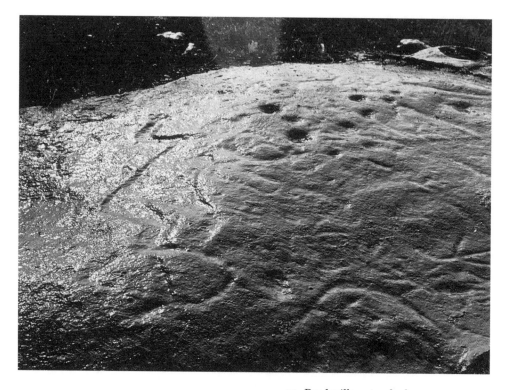

17. Reedyville petroglyphs.

18. Drawing of Reedyville petroglyphs.

19. Circle with cross petroglyph at Reedyville.

CARTER CAVES PICTOGRAPH SITE (15CR60)

LOCATION: Carter County, northeast of Riggs Hill on the Grahn Quadrangle. This site is not in Carter Caves proper. Elevation: 230 m (740 ft).

DESCRIPTION: Figure 20 portrays the pictograph as seen from the north. Two pictographs, a geometric design and a human foot, are visible at the base of a limestone cliff face. The geometric design averages about 55 cm (22 in) across and about 45 cm (18 in) from top to bottom. It is a rectangular to oval outline enclosing an equal arm cross. The diameter of the enclosed cross measures 56 cm (22.4 in) horizontally and 45.5 cm (18.2 in) vertically. The human footprint measures nearly 0.6 m (2 ft) from toe to heel. The pigment used in both figures is gone, but the pigment used initially apparently has had an inhibitory action on the dark algae that covers the cliff face. The resulting image resembles a photographic negative with a colorless image superimposed on a dark background.

20. View of the limestone cliff face bearing the Carter Caves pictographs.

21. View of the Carter Caves pictograph.

This is one of the two known pictograph sites we classified as Native American in Kentucky, the other being the Asphalt Rock Pictographs (15ED24). It is also the only example of limestone being used as a canvas. Coy, Fuller, Meadows, and John Tierney, the Carter Caves Resort Park employee who served as a guide, believe this is Native American in origin. Swauger is less convinced because the mode and technique differs from the style of other sites studied. The enclosed cross design is similar in appearance to a Late Prehistoric (A.D. 1000–1600) motif known as a "sun circle".

BIBLIOGRAPHIC SOURCES: Funkhouser and Webb 1932.

FIRST RECORDED BY AUTHORS: Coy and Fuller, May 1972.

PILOT ROCK PETROGLYPH SITE (15CH200)

LOCATION: Christian County, atop the well-known Pilot Rock, plainly delineated on the Honey Grove Quadrangle southwest of Flat Rock School and northeast of Ebenezer Church. Elevation: 294 m (966 ft).

DESCRIPTION: The petroglyphs were observed on a small sandstone ledge on the western side and near the summit of Pilot Rock (Fig. 22). This site was

22. Bird tracks at Pilot Rock.

first described by Sanders (1977), who noted "a dozen good hominy holes, 2 or 3 'abrading' areas, several (at least 3) turkey tracks (1 possibly with rich red ocher paint); & a series of concentric circles plus numerous small cupular pits or nutting areas." Swauger's examination suggested that the bird tracks had been produced by rubbing alone. He could not determine if red ocher paint had been applied. Sanders and Maynard (1979, 220) included several badly disturbed rockshelters as part of this site. No diagnostic artifacts were recovered from the site, making it impossible to assess cultural affiliation.

BIBLIOGRAPHIC SOURCES: Sanders 1977; Sanders and Maynard 1979.

BAR CREEK PETROGLYPH SITE (15CY18)

LOCATION: Clay County, north of Spurlock and south of the Red Bird River, on the Barcreek Quadrangle. Elevation: 256 m (840 ft).

23. View of the Bar Creek rockshelter (George I. Hensley pictured).

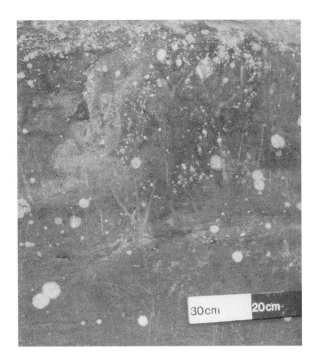

24. Bird tracks at the Bar Creek rockshelter.

DESCRIPTION: The petroglyphs are located on the exterior western face of the rockshelter rather than the interior, where petroglyphs typically occur. The designs include three bird tracks with center toes an average of 9 cm (3.6 in) in length. Figures 23 and 24 illustrate the site and its contents. The designs are shallow but have a fairly sharp "V"-shaped cross section that is somewhat unusual among Native American petroglyphs. Because of the sharpness of the cross sections, the Native American origins of this site are questionable.

BIBLIOGRAPHIC SOURCES: None are known.

FIRST RECORDED BY AUTHORS: Coy and Fuller, November 1971.

RED BIRD RIVER PETROGLYPH SITE (15CY51)

LOCATION: Clay County, in a sandstone cliff on the bank of the Red Bird River, north of the New Berry School on the Big Creek Quadrangle. Elevation: 310 m (1020 ft).

DESCRIPTION: Coy and Fuller (1969b) described this site:

25. View of the Red Bird River
petroglyph site.

Red Bird River and Goose Creek together form the headwaters of the South
Fork of the Kentucky River, joining at Oneida in Clay County, Kentucky. Nine
and one-half miles upstream, State Highway 66 has recently been built on the
northeast bank of Red Bird River, 30 feet or so above the river and at the base
of a 60 foot cliff. Here the Kentucky State Historical Society has erected a historical marker with the following inscription:

> "CHIEF RED BIRD was a legendary Cherokee Indian for whom this
> fork of the Kentucky River is named. He and another Indian, Jack,
> whose name was given to the creek to the south, were friendly with
> early settlers and permitted to hunt in this area. Allegedly they were
> killed in battle protecting their furs and the bodies thrown into the
> river here. The ledges bear markings attributed to Red Bird."

We first heard of this from Michael Hensley of Oneida, who having been
stimulated by a paper on Kentucky petroglyphs by one of us (Fuller 1969b),
visited the site and found the "markings" still clearly visible. At his invitation
we too examined the site and found the carvings on a vertical face of sandstone 16 feet above the road.

26. The Red Bird River petroglyphs.

27. Drawing of the Red Bird River
petroglyphs.

The surface was relatively flat, measuring 1.6 m (5.5 ft) in height and 6 m (20 ft) in length. The many carvings were sharply incised and linear in design (Figs. 26, 27) After inspecting the area, it appeared that Kentucky Highway 66 was graded to a lower level than the original ground surface. This was confirmed by Mr. Hensley, who told us that only a trail had existed previously. An estimate of the original surface would place the carvings at chest height.

These carvings were different from any of the previously reported Kentucky petroglyphs (Mallery 1893; Bushnell 1913; Weller 1927; Funkhouser and Webb 1932; Coy and Fuller 1966, 1967, and 1968; Fuller 1969a and 1969b) in that they were made up of sharply incised straight lines.

No mention of Chief Red Bird could be found in several early Kentucky histories published in the nineteenth century. Therefore we contacted the Kentucky Historical Society and received the following letter (Wentworth 1969): "You will note that on our marker we say that he was a legendary Cherokee Indian. There is much legend in the area, but very little of any specific nature and no reliable dates are available. The only thing that we can do is guess that it occurred probably about 1780–1800. That was when settlers were first coming into the area there, although they were very sparse."

A series of well-preserved linear carvings on a sandstone ledge extending from the face of a small cliff in Clay County, Kentucky, has been described. The antiquity of this petroglyph has not been established, but the legend concerning their origin has been alluded to.

BIBLIOGRAPHIC SOURCES: Coy and Fuller 1969b, 1970b; Funkhouser and Webb 1932; Wentworth 1969.

FIRST RECORDED BY AUTHORS: Coy and Fuller, September 1969.

RED BIRD RIVER SHELTER PETROGLYPH SITE (15CY52)

LOCATION: Clay County, on the west bank of the Red Bird River, south of Brutus Church and north of New Berry School, on the Big Creek Quadrangle. Elevation: 290 m (950 ft).

DESCRIPTION: The rockshelter faces south (Figs. 28, 29). It is approximately 2 m (6.6 ft) wide at the mouth, constricts to a passageway 1.5 m (5 ft) in width, and then opens into a room 3 m (10 ft) in width. The total depth of the rockshelter is 5 m (16.5 ft). The designs were pounded, rubbed, and cut into sandstone. Petroglyphs are generally clustered toward the rockshelter opening on both sides. The design elements consist of linear incisions and several bird tracks, overlain by modern graffiti. Figures 30 and 31 show the eastern and western walls, looking south from the rockshelter opening as seen during a 1969 visit. The figures illustrate the placement of the carvings near the entrance where light is most intense. Figure 32 illustrates the east wall dur-

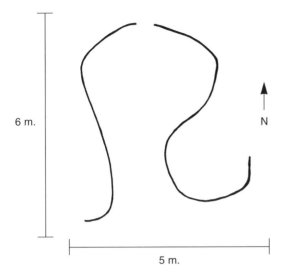

6 m.

5 m.

N

28. Plan of the Red Bird River rockshelter.

29. View of the entrance of the Red Bird River rockshelter.

30. Petroglyphs on the east wall of the Red Bird River rockshelter.

31. Petroglyphs on the west wall of the Red Bird River rockshelter.

32. View of the Red Bird River rockshelter petroglyphs showing the post-1969 addition of a human face.

ing a 1993 visit; note the addition of a human face that was not present in 1969.

Native American petroglyphs are plentiful at this site, including bird tracks and sharpening grooves mingled with numerous modern initials and dates for the most part. The Historic petroglyphs are cut sharply with straight-line cross sections typical of marks made by metal tools (Swauger 1974). Other straight-line designs have blunter, wider, and shallower cross sections, which led Swauger to classify them as Native American tool-sharpening grooves. The assignment as Native American or Euro-American is subjective, but we believe the Red Bird River Shelter Site is a genuine Native American petroglyph site extensively overlain with modern graffiti.

BIBLIOGRAPHIC SOURCES: None is known.

FIRST RECORDED BY AUTHORS: Coy and Fuller, September 1969.

FISH TRAP ROCK PETROGLYPH SITE (15CY53)

LOCATION: Clay County, on the west bank of the Red Bird River, southeast of New Berry School on the Big Creek Quadrangle. Bridge construction necessitated its movement from its original position. Figure 33 illustrates the size of the petroglyph rock and its present relation to the river and the bridge. Elevation: 290 m (950 ft).

DESCRIPTION: The designs of the Fish Trap Rock Site were pounded and rubbed into a large sandstone boulder, measuring approximately 3.5 m (11.6 ft) in length and 2–3 m (6.6–10 ft) in width (Fig. 33). The petroglyphs occur on a smooth, rounded upper surface (Fig. 34). There are an estimated 20–25 bird tracks present but none were observed to overlap. Because of weathering, the designs have become quite shallow and virtually impossible to discern in direct light. By a serendipitous set of circumstances, we viewed the rock in low light conditions, which heightened the contrast of the markings and allowed them to be examined. However, these lighting conditions made an accurate count extremely difficult.

33. View of the Fish Trap Rock.

34. Bird tracks on the Fish Trap Rock.

The tracks at the site are typical of many other examples documented in the state except for the presence of two lines or bars placed on either side and at right angles to the "spur" (the single line emanating from the juncture of the toes).

BIBLIOGRAPHIC SOURCES: None is known.

FIRST RECORDED BY AUTHORS: Coy and Fuller, September 1971.

LAUREL BRANCH PETROGLYPH SITE (15CY265)

LOCATION: Clay County, on an unnamed branch of Laurel Creek, east of Goose Creek on the Bar Creek Quadrangle. Elevation: 310 m (1020 ft).

DESCRIPTION: This site is a small rockshelter under a waterfall (Fig. 35). Linear marks (Fig. 36) were observed on a diamond-shaped boulder with sides measuring 0.85, 1.35, 1.08, and 1.06 m (34, 54, 43, and 42.5 in). The boulder is 62.5 cm (25 in) in thickness. The rock was probably part of the rockshelter roof when the marks were made.

BIBLIOGRAPHIC SOURCES: None is known.

FIRST RECORDED BY AUTHORS: Coy and Fuller, October 1993.

35. View of the Laurel Branch petro-glyph site (Tom Fuller pictured).

36. Petroglyphs at Laurel Branch.

DISMAL ROCK PETROGLYPH SITE (15ED15)

LOCATION: Edmonson County, south of Kyrock Church on the Bee Spring Quadrangle, on the right bank of the Nolin River. Elevation: 170 m (550 ft).

DESCRIPTION: Douglas W. Schwartz (1960, 10) first described this site in a survey report of sites in the Nolin River reservoir area. He included within the site definition a cave containing the petroglyphs, an adjoining ledge and a campsite 60 m (200 ft) west of the Nolin River. He also noted that the cave held water during wet weather, leaving only the vestibule suitable for habitation. The petroglyphs were described as "coiled snakes and turkey tracks." Several artifacts were recovered from the campsite and a single artifact was collected from the ledge, but no cultural affiliation could be assigned to the site. Later visits by the authors confirmed and augmented Schwartz's observations.

The petroglyphs are carved on the face of a large block of sandstone roof fall that leans against the north wall of the cave (Fig. 37). Two spirals were

37. View of the Dismal Rock petroglyph site.

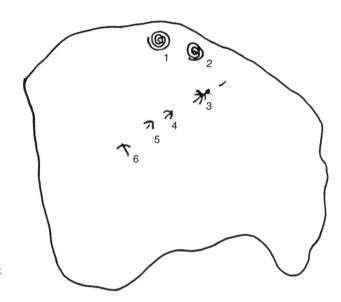

38. Drawing of petroglyphs at Dismal Rock.

noted in the top central portion of the ledge (nos. 1 and 2, Fig. 38). The higher spiral is slightly less than 20 cm (8 in) at its greatest diameter, the lower slightly more than 10 cm (4 in). At least four "bird tracks" descend from below the second spiral to the left as one views the drawing (nos. 3–6, Fig. 38). The designs were all pecked into the rock and display practically no traces of rubbing.

BIBLIOGRAPHIC SOURCES: Schwartz 1960; Fuller 1969a.

FIRST RECORDED BY AUTHORS: Coy and Fuller, June 1969.

ASPHALT ROCK PICTOGRAPHS SITE (15ED24)

LOCATION: Edmonson County, southwest of New Liberty Church on the Brownsville Quadrangle. Elevation: 170 m (550 ft).

DESCRIPTION: The pictographs of the Asphalt Rock Site were painted on sandstone. They are found in one of three rockshelters at the base of the line of cliffs beneath the plateau that overlooks the Green River Valley (Fig. 39). The middle rockshelter containing the paintings is 45 m (148.5 ft) in length, 9 m (29.7 ft) in depth, 4.5 m (14.9 ft) high and faces southwest. The pictographs

39. View of the Asphalt Rock pictograph site.

cover an area measuring 0.96 m (3.2 ft) high by 1.37 m (4.5 ft) long on the back wall of the rockshelter, 2.4 m (7.9 ft) above the floor. The rockshelter has been extensively dug by people presumably hunting artifacts, but, surprisingly enough, there has been no defacement of the paintings. In the debris left behind from the diggings are found many pieces of worked flint, cordmarked, grit-tempered pottery shards, freshwater mussel shells, and several animal bone fragments. The pictographs occur on the upper portion of the rear wall, which is relatively smooth and appears to be unweathered. The wall surface below the pictographs shows evidence of recent spalling. During the authors' first visit to the site, a rainstorm was in progress. Despite moderate winds, the rockshelter area remained quite dry and rain did not reach the back wall.

The pictographs are mostly a dull red in color and include both stylized representational and abstract drawings (Figs. 40, 41). The stylized representational subject is that of a human, probably male, with his arms held at right angles from the shoulder and flexed at the elbow with the hands above the

40. Asphalt Rock pictographs.

41. Drawing of the Asphalt Rock pictographs.

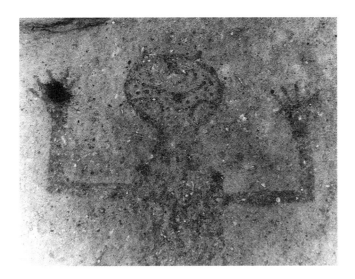

42. Stylized human figure at Asphalt Rock.

head (Fig. 42). A deep red pigment was used that is well preserved above the arms but fades toward the lower body. Two horn-like projections and a cat-like mask or facial painting are observable on the head and face. The remainder of the body and arms appear to be solid, but weathering has obscured the lower portion of the painting and may have obliterated additional body parts or other designs.

One of the abstract drawings is a large circle, 41 cm (1.4 ft) in diameter, with several geometric figures within its circumference (Fig. 43). Some of the geometric elements appear to be placed inside zones delimited by curvilinear lines. Beneath the circle is an hourglass-shaped figure measuring 15 by 27 cm (6 by 10.8 in). Lines enclose the circle and hourglass-shaped figure on each site but do not close at the top and bottom. Beneath this motif are portions of two concentric lines. Both of these motifs retain deep red pigment and bold lines.

Between the two larger motifs are two smaller, indistinct drawings. One appears to be a small drawing of a human head and torso executed in narrow lines. The other is a birdlike figure in a lighter red color. All of the paintings are primarily monochromatic, except that the abstract figures may have been outlined with a darker pigment that has since been reduced by weathering to a faint stain.

This site is outstanding because it is one of only two well-documented pictograph localities that still survive in the state. Pictographs have been reported from many of the surrounding states including Indiana (McMurtrie 1819),

43. Circular and hourglass motifs at Asphalt Rock.

Illinois (Peithman 1952), Missouri (Brownlee 1956; Diesing and Magre 1942), and Tennessee (Cambron and Waters 1959; Parker 1948). Funkhouser and Webb (1932, 76) reported the presence of a pictograph in the Carter Caves area in Carter County, Kentucky.

Analysis of the pigment used to execute the paintings revealed that the red color was produced from natural ochre and the black was probably from a carbonaceous source (Kingery 1982). The analyst was very certain that the pigments were not modern. Given these observations and the nature of the paintings themselves as well as the presence of cultural midden in the rock-shelter, we are reasonably confident that these renderings represent the work of prehistoric Native Americans.

BIBLIOGRAPHIC SOURCES: Coy and Fuller 1969; Fuller 1969a.

FIRST RECORDED BY AUTHORS: Coy and Fuller, March 1969.

LITTLE FAIRDALE PETROGLYPH SITE (15ED96)

LOCATION: Edmonson County, southwest of the Nolin River and north of the Cove Hollow Church, on the Nolin Reservoir Quadrangle. Elevation: about 200 m (660 ft).

DESCRIPTION: This site consists of a sandstone boulder in an open field (Fig. 44). The exposed surface of the rock measures 0.6 m (2 ft) in diameter and is flush with the ground. Two bird tracks are carved on this surface, one quite obvious and the other somewhat obscured. The longitudinal axes of these tracks appear to point to rockshelter areas, with bedrock mortars, about 180 m (600 ft) distant on the bluffs overlooking Nolin River (Coy and Fuller 1966).

BIBLIOGRAPHIC SOURCES: Coy and Fuller 1966.

FIRST RECORDED BY AUTHORS: Coy and Fuller, June 1964.

44. View of the Little Fairdale petroglyph site.

BIG GIMLET PETROGLYPH SITE (15EL3)

LOCATION: Elliott County, in a sandstone rockshelter on the northeast side of Big Gimlet Creek, west of Access and north of Grundy Church, on the Bruin Quadrangle. Elevation: about 240 m (800 ft).

DESCRIPTION: The rockshelter housing the petroglyphs is enormous, and the boulders holding the designs are not immediately observable (Fig. 45). The rockshelter measures approximately 93 m (310 ft) across its opening and as deep as 42 m (140 ft). The sandstone roof fall on which most of the designs are carved is about 4.2 m (14 ft) south of the lip of the overhang near the eastern point of its sweep (Fig. 45). The lip of the overhang is about 19.8 m (66 ft) above the petroglyphs. Approximately 3.6 m (12 ft) east of this main rock is another boulder on whose southern rim is carved a bird track.

Figure 46 illustrates the seven bird tracks visible on the rock bearing the greatest number of designs. The tracks are close together and, in some

45. View of the Big Gimlet petroglyph site.

46. Tracks at Big Gimlet.

instances, overlap. East of the line of bird tracks, and heading in a southeasterly direction, is a set of paw prints. We called them rabbit tracks.

A lone bird track was documented on the rock east of the one with the other designs. It appears to have been produced by pecking. Remnants of the arcs of its initial forming are still clear. The northern face of this petroglyph rock also bears a series of somewhat ovular holes of uncertain origin.

BIBLIOGRAPHIC SOURCES: None is known.

FIRST RECORDED BY AUTHORS: Coy, Fuller, and Meadows, May 1972.

SPARKS INDIAN ROCK HOUSE PETROGLYPH SITE (15ES26)

LOCATION: Estill County, southeast of Double Oak Cemetery on the Leighton Quadrangle. The site is also known as the Granny Richards Rock House, presumably because of the proximity of the Granny Richards Springs School. Elevation: about 370 m (1,200 ft).

DESCRIPTION: This is a rockshelter containing numerous boulders and roof fall (Fig. 47). Native American carvings were documented on five boulders in

47. View of the Sparks Indian Rock House petroglyph site.

48. Drawing showing locations of the petroglyph-bearing boulders in the Sparks Indian Rock House.

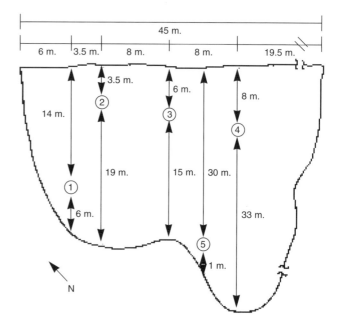

49. Boulder #1 showing rayed circle and grooves in the Sparks Indian Rock House.

the eastern half of the rockshelter. The carved boulders are numbered in Figure 48.

Boulder no. 1 is about 1 m (3.3 ft) in maximum length, just under 90 cm (3 ft) at greatest width, and projects nearly 90 cm (3 ft) above the ground. It contains three heads, a portion of a rayed circle, and a number of grooves that may or may not be Native American (Fig. 49). The three heads (Fig. 50), skele-

50. Head motif on Boulder #1 in the Sparks Indian Rock House.

tal in nature, are on the west-southwestern portion of the boulder. The heads were pounded out in shallow, relatively broad grooves as much as 6 cm (2.4 in) wide. The eyes and mouths were gouged out by pecking. The heads appear less weathered than the other designs, which casts some doubt on their Native American origin. The rayed circle is in the northern section of the boulder. One of the rays terminates with a small rounded element (Fig. 51). It is possible that someone attempted to carve a bird track on the rock east of the highest carved head. However, the sharpness of its "V"-shaped profile makes us reluctant to accept it as Native American.

Boulder no. 2 contains two human feet and a human hand print (Fig. 52). There are other markings on the boulder, notably "V" shapes, but the feet and the hand are the most noticeable, and the only ones we accept as Native American manufacture.

The main features of Boulder no. 3 are a vulva form and a human stick figure on the northern arc of the rock. Figures 53, 54, and 55 illustrate these features, their sizes, and their relationships to each other. There are numerous other marks on the rock, including Euro-American initials and several pecked and incised designs. Some of these may be Native American; however, in at least one instance (Figs. 53, 56), the "P" of a set of initials "E.P" was converted to a bird track between 1970 and 1984.

A "rayed" head was recorded on Boulder no. 4 (Fig. 57). It appears that the original "head" and some other elements were produced by a Native American but that the rays were added later.

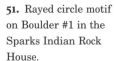

51. Rayed circle motif on Boulder #1 in the Sparks Indian Rock House.

52. Human foot- and hand prints on Boulder #2 in the Sparks Indian Rock House.

53. Boulder #3 showing vulva form and human stick figure in the Sparks Indian Rock House (note the unaltered initials "E.P." above the vulva form).

54. Vulva form motif on Boulder #3 in the Sparks Indian Rock House.

55. Human stick figure on Boulder #3 in the Sparks Indian Rock House.

56. Boulder #3 showing initials "E.P."
converted to a bird track at the Sparks
Indian Rock House.

57. Rayed head motif on Boulder #4 in
the Sparks Indian Rock House.

Boulder no. 5 (Fig. 58) contains a small human footprint and a series of five pits in a circular pattern.

Other rocks in the rockshelter may bear Native American designs, but none is certain and, in the case of some lines and arcs, may be natural, Native American, or Euro-American.

We have reservations about the rayed circle on Boulder no. 1. The body of the design, the circle, is probably of Native American manufacture because of its generally rubbed appearance, although one must be aware, as well, that circles of this sort are sometimes produced by natural agencies (Swauger 1984, 244–46). The rays are a different matter. They exhibit sharply cut "V"-shaped profiles, rather than having the more typical "U"-shaped cross sec-

58. Boulder #5 showing the human footprint (beneath the scale) and the five pits in the Sparks Indian Rock House.

tions that we accept as evidence of Native American manufacture (Swauger 1974, 99). Even the small rounded element at the end of one of the rays is suspect as it seems to incorporate both a "U"-shaped and a sharply cut, "V"-shaped cross section. In any event, we decided that the circle is Native American. The lower quarter or so of the circle of the design has spalled from the rock.

There is no reason to doubt the Native American origin of the vulva design on Boulder no. 3, which is similar to an example from West Virginia (Swauger 1974, 83, pl. 95). The stick figure's lines are narrow and sharp but were produced by pecking and rubbing, so it is acceptable as a Native American design.

The rays on the head of Boulder no. 4 are much sharper than the outlines of the head and circle and other pitted forms on the rock, so much so that we feel that they were produced with a metal tool. If this is the case, the argument against a Native American origin of the rays of the rayed circle on Boulder no. 1 is strengthened. The character of the pecking of the head and other features of Boulder no. 4 is different from the designs on Boulder no. 1, but what that may mean, we do not know.

BIBLIOGRAPHIC SOURCES: None is known.

FIRST RECORDED BY AUTHORS: Coy, Fuller, and Meadows, October 1970.

ASHLEY PETROGLYPH SITE (15ES27)

LOCATION: Estill County, north of the Mountain Spring School and northeast of the Watson School, on the Cob Hill Quadrangle. Elevation: about 370 m (1,200 ft).

DESCRIPTION: The site is a north-facing rockshelter measuring 6 m (19.8 ft) in height and 16.2 m (53.5 ft) in width at the entrance (Fig. 59). The greatest breadth of arc from the line of the entrance is 12.2 m (40.3 ft). A panel of six bird tracks is observable at the base of the south wall. Figure 60 illustrates the form and distribution of the site's designs. The tracks are rather randomly distributed and do not appear to point to any particular feature.

BIBLIOGRAPHIC SOURCES: None is known.

FIRST RECORDED BY AUTHORS: Coy and Fuller, April 1984.

59. View of the Ashley petroglyph site (Tom Fuller pictured).

60. Ashley petroglyphs (Johnny Faulkner pictured).

SPARKS II PETROGLYPH SITE (15ES59)

LOCATION: Estill County, on a ridgetop saddle near the Sparks Indian Rock House on the Leighton Quadrangle. Elevation: 400 m (1,310 ft).

DESCRIPTION: The petroglyphs at this site consist of at least two human footprints that have been pecked into an exposed rock outcrop (Fig. 61). One of the prints is almost obliterated by weathering. The second print is outlined with a circle that appears to be of recent date (Fig. 62).

BIBLIOGRAPHIC SOURCES: None is known.

FIRST RECORDED BY AUTHORS: Coy, May 1987.

61. Rock outcrop at the Sparks II petroglyph site, showing human footprints (Tom Fuller pictured).

62. Human footprint with more recent circle surrounding it in the Sparks II petroglyph site.

CROW HOLLOW PETROGLYPH SITE (15GY65)

LOCATION: Grayson County, northeast of West Clifty and south of Goodman School, on the Big Clifty Quadrangle. Elevation: 180 m (600 ft).

DESCRIPTION: This site is a rockshelter containing two sections of a boulder that bear Native American petroglyphs (Figs. 63, 64). The northerly section bears clear carvings reasonably identifiable as rabbit tracks between more northwesterly and centrally located paw tracks defined as raccoon (Fig. 65). The more southerly section (Fig. 66) bears a clear bird track.

Both boulders exhibit shallow elements, for instance, five abrasions resembling star points southwest of the tip of the bird track on the more southerly rock and pecked elements to its northeastern and southeastern areas. Some might interpret these markings as Native American designs modified by changes brought on by the passage of time, but we prefer to define

63. View of the Crow Hollow petroglyph site.

only the elements identified as raccoon, rabbit, and bird tracks as surely created by Native Americans. A small bedrock mortar was present on the rock
with the petroglyphs.

BIBLIOGRAPHIC SOURCES: None is known.

FIRST RECORDED BY AUTHORS: Coy and Fuller, March 1970.

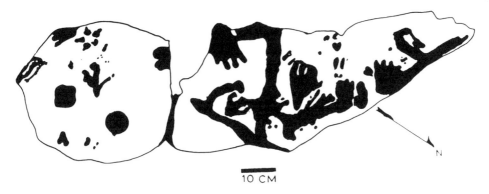

64. Drawing of petroglyphs at Crow Hollow.

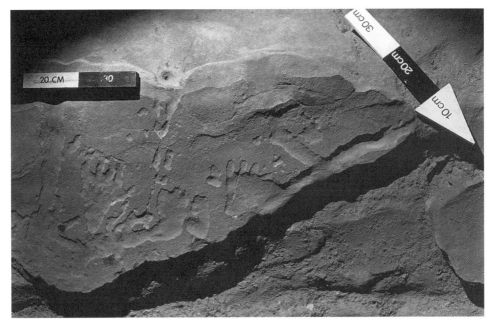

65. Northerly boulder at Crow Hollow showing rabbit and raccoon tracks.

66. Southerly boulder at Crow Hollow showing bird track.

SALTSMAN BRANCH PETROGLYPH SITE (15GY66)

LOCATION: Grayson County, south of Moutardier and southeast of McGrew Church, on the Bee Spring Quadrangle. Elevation: about 200 m (650 ft).

DESCRIPTION: This site consists of a sandstone rock outcrop in a roadbed running along a ridge saddle (Fig. 67). The designs were pecked and rubbed into a sheet of rock sparsely covered with grass and much scarred by the passage

67. View of the Saltsman Branch petroglyph
site (Tom Fuller pictured).

of vehicles. Twelve bird and three deer tracks were identified by Weller (1927,
166–68). Swauger later documented an isolated bird track west of the two
groups. Figure 68 illustrates the designs of the site and their relationship to
each other, according to Weller.

This site was visited several times between 1967 and 1985 and exempli-
fies the changes in clarity that weathering causes. The bird track west of the
main group of tracks was quite clear on all three visits. On the other hand,
while by no means indiscernible, the main group of bird tracks was not as
clear in 1984 as it had been in earlier years. This may have been a function of
the lighting conditions on each visit, but we know from talking with the owner,
L.M. Harrison, and his son, Leon Harrison, that there has been considerable
wheeled traffic over the rock in recent years. Were one to view the markings
under a variety of lighting conditions, one could determine under which con-

68. Weller's 1927 illustration of the Saltsman Branch petroglyphs. Used with permission of the Kentucky Geological Survey.

ditions the tracks would be more distinct, but it is likely that erosion by traffic has significantly and negatively affected the clarity of the markings.

BIBLIOGRAPHIC SOURCES: Coy 1991, 1993, 1994; Weller 1927.

FIRST RECORDED BY AUTHORS: Coy and Fuller, March 1970.

SALTSMAN BRANCH SHELTER PETROGLYPH SITE (15GY66)

LOCATION: Grayson County, northeast of BM 700, and west of BM 797, on the Nolin Reservoir Quadrangle. Elevation: 200 m (650 ft).

DESCRIPTION: This site is a relatively small, south-facing sandstone rockshelter, measuring 90 m (297 ft) in width, 30 m (99 ft) in depth and 15 m (49.5 ft) in height (Fig. 69). Two areas of designs were documented, including seven bird tracks pecked and rubbed into a rock near the opening of the rockshelter's western boundary, and an abrading area for the shaping and sharpening of edged tools on the west northwest wall. Figure 70 illustrates the shape and dimensions of the rockshelter, locates the rock bearing the bird tracks, and indicates the approximate size of the abrading area as well.

As seen in Figures 70 and 71, the tracks were clustered along the curve of the rock at the entrance to the rockshelter. The abrading area is located along the northeast arc of the rockshelter and covers part of a ledge and extends up to the base of the wall that curves over the ledge. It includes seven linear incisions and another bird track (Fig. 71). The bird tracks are clear and appear quite typical. The "toes" of the tracks are all oriented toward the outside of the rockshelter.

BIBLIOGRAPHIC SOURCES: None is known.

FIRST RECORDED BY AUTHORS: Coy and Fuller, July 1967.

69. View of the Saltsman Branch rockshelter.

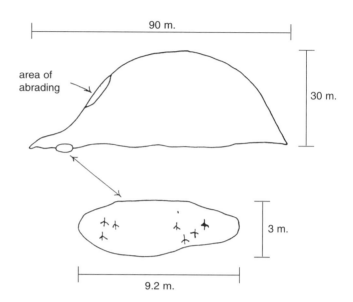

70. Drawing of the Saltsman Branch rockshelter showing locations of the petroglyphs.

71. Bird tracks on the rock at the entrance to the Saltsman Branch rockshelter.

JEFFRY CLIFF PETROGLYPH SITE (15HA114)

LOCATION: Hancock County, north of Sunny Corner on the Cloverport Quadrangle. Elevation: about 170 m (550 ft).

DESCRIPTION: This site is a large northwestern-facing rockshelter with a semicircular floor plan, first documented by the University of Kentucky in 1979 (Turnbow et al. 1980) (Fig. 72). Petroglyphs were documented in three distinct clusters. Two clusters were located in the main portion of the rockshelter. One of the clusters consisted of four separate designs on a moderate sized boulder. According to Turnbow et al. (1980, 217), the designs (Fig. 74) included:

> (1) a rounded square with two U-shaped elements inside (20 cm by 13 cm) [8 by 5.2 in], (2) two U-shaped elements (11 cm by 10 cm) [4.4 by 4 in], (3) one design with a scroll and S-shaped element (7 cm by 7 cm) [2.8 by 2.8 in], and (4) a partly broken off design with a scroll and S-shaped element (15 cm by 12 cm) [6 by 4.8 in]. The designs are grouped together on the boulder, placed less than 35 cm apart.

72. View of the Jeffry Cliff petroglyph site.

73. Drawing of petro-
glyphs in Area B of the
Jeffry Cliff petroglyph
site.

74. Petroglyphs in Area B of Jeffry Cliff.

Another cluster included six straight lines pecked into a large rock on the floor at the northeastern edge. The petroglyph measures 20 cm by 30 cm (8 by 12 in). Each line is 2.5 cm to 3 cm (1–1.2 in) wide and less than 12 cm (4.8 in) long (Turnbow, et al. 1980, 217–18). The third cluster was located on a separate boulder and included:

> three straight lines and an eroded semicircle. . . . The straight lines are 2.5 cm to 3 cm [1–1.2 in] wide and 10 cm [4 in] long. The semicircle is 10 cm [4 in] in diameter. A bedrock mortar on the same boulder is 8 cm [3.2 in] in diameter and over 10 cm [4 in] deep. The mortar is only 5 cm [2 in] from Petroglyph 3, raising the possibility that it might have functioned in the activity related to the mortar. (Turnbow, et al. 1980, 217–18)

A fourth possible petroglyph was also documented as a badly weathered curvilinear element.

BIBLIOGRAPHIC SOURCES: Turnbow, et al. 1980.

FIRST RECORDED BY AUTHORS: Coy, January 1987.

DAUGHERTY BEAR TRACK PETROGLYPH SITE (15JA160)

LOCATION: Jackson County, west of Dry Fork School and southeast of Corinth Church on the Johnetta Quadrangle. Elevation: 370 m (1,200 ft).

DESCRIPTION: This site is a sandstone outcrop on the side of a ravine, facing almost due west about 30 m (100 ft) above a freshwater spring (Fig. 75). The petroglyphs cover an area measuring 3.3 by 5.1 m (11 by 17 ft). Twenty-one paw prints (identified as bear), one small and two large circles, and a zig-zag linear design were carved into the rock (Fig. 76).

The circle in the southwestern area of the group of designs (Fig. 76) is typical of all three circles at the site. Its channel varies from nearly 4 cm (1.6 in) to about 1.5 cm (0.6 in) in width. It was produced by pounding and rubbing and has a hole in its center. The four paws associated with it on the south side are oriented to the north. The paw print almost due north of the circle is oriented to the southeast. The four prints beyond the linear design are oriented to the northeast. The zig-zag linear figure (Fig. 77) to the northeast of the circle is similar to designs identified as stick-figure animals at sites such as the Indian God Rock Site (CMNH-36VE26) on the Allegheny River in Venango

75. View of Daugherty Bear Track petroglyph site.

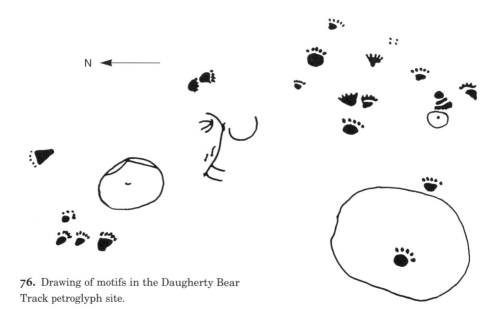

76. Drawing of motifs in the Daugherty Bear
Track petroglyph site.

77. Zig-zag linear figure in the Daugherty Bear Track petroglyph site.

County, Pennsylvania (Swauger 1974, 75, plate 107). The line curving north-west from the northern arc of the circle is natural.

The paw prints documented at this site may be intended to represent bear tracks. The fact that circles enclose four of the tracks may have meant something to the carvers but, if so, we have no clue as to what. There is a purpose-fully carved hole in the approximate center of the small circle in the southwest area of the carved area, almost as if it had been made by the pointed leg of a compass used to draw a circle.

BIBLIOGRAPHIC SOURCES: None is known.

FIRST RECORDED BY AUTHORS: Coy and Fuller, January 1971.

BRUSHY RIDGE PETROGLYPH SITE (15JA161)

LOCATION: Jackson County, north of Sparks School on the McKee Quadrangle. Elevation: about 450 m (1,480 ft).

DESCRIPTION: Petroglyphs were documented on the southern arc and the westerly curve of the wall of a small sandstone rockshelter (Fig. 78). The rock-

78. View of the Brushy Ridge
petroglyph site.

shelter measures 4.5 by 6 m (20 by 15 ft) and is 2.25 m (7.5 ft) high. The
designs include bird and animal tracks and, in at least one instance, an arc of
dots that could have been a first step in the carving of another animal paw
(Fig. 79). The bird tracks are to the west along the wall, consisting of a line of
five tracks on the rear wall above the floor, and a single track also on the wall
but higher than the group (Fig. 80). The bird track lines in several instances
are very sharp, but it is conjectured that rubbing with a hard and well-shaped
stone celt could produce such a result.

The animal tracks are limited to two complete examples and one possible
partial tract. The two complete tracks are clustered together (Fig. 81).

BIBLIOGRAPHIC SOURCES: None is known.

FIRST RECORDED BY AUTHORS: Coy, November 1979.

79. Drawing of petroglyphs in Brushy Ridge.

80. Bird tracks in Brushy Ridge.

81. Complete paw prints in Brushy Ridge.

WILLIAM GAY PETROGLYPH SITE (15JA234)

LOCATION: Jackson County, on a small knoll along a southeasterly trending ridge separating the Middle Fork and Lime Kiln drainages on the McKee Quadrangle. Elevation: 560 m (1,340 ft).

DESCRIPTION: The petroglyphs are carved into a sandstone outcrop near the southeast end of the knoll (Fig. 82). They include nine bear tracks, two human footprints, and two footprints that seem to combine human and bear characteristics (Fig. 83). A single deer track is also present.

BIBLIOGRAPHIC SOURCES: None is known.

FIRST RECORDED BY AUTHORS: Coy, January 1988.

82. View of the William Gay petroglyph site (Emily Coy pictured).

83. Drawing of tracks and prints at William Gay.

CHRISTMAS EVE PETROGLYPH SITE (15JA235)

LOCATION: Jackson County, west of the Cavanaugh School on the Sandgap Quadrangle. Elevation: 430 m (1,400 ft).

DESCRIPTION: The designs are carved into a sandstone boulder in a large rockshelter about 18 m (60 ft) across at the mouth, 9 m (30 ft) in height, and 12–18 m (40–60 ft) deep (Fig. 84). The boulder, measuring about 90 cm (3 ft) in diameter, exhibited about 25 split-hoof animal tracks of various shapes (Fig. 85). Traces of former nitre mining operations are observable.

BIBLIOGRAPHIC SOURCES: None is known.

FIRST RECORDED BY AUTHORS: Coy and Meadows, January 1987.

84. View of the Christmas Eve petroglyph site.

85. Boulder bearing petroglyphs in the Christmas Eve site.

PETER CAVE BRANCH PETROGLYPH SITE (15JA355)

LOCATION: Jackson County, southeast of the Flat Top Church on Peter Cave Branch, on the Parrot Quadrangle. Elevation: 310 m (1,020 ft).

DESCRIPTION: Peter Cave Branch is a large rockshelter with many grottoes (Fig. 86). Disturbed archaeological deposits dating to the Late Woodland period have been identified here by U.S. Forest Service archaeologist Cecil Ison. A panel of petroglyphs was recorded on a section of rear wall, starting at ground level and covering a square meter (Fig. 87). Identified petroglyphs include two human footprints, one bear track, at least eight bird tracks and three small tracks that may be mink or squirrel (Fig. 88). Numerous abrading marks, some superimposed on the footprints, were observed. An abraded area on the upper right side of the panel resembles an inverted comma. The cave also has many historic initials.

BIBLIOGRAPHIC SOURCES: None is known.

FIRST RECORDED BY AUTHORS: Coy, May 1993.

86. View of Peter Cave.

87. Rock face containing petroglyphs in
Peter Cave.

88. Closeup of small tracks adjacent to
the footprint in Peter Cave.

BIG TURTLE SHELTER PETROGLYPH SITE (15LE55)

LOCATION: Lee County, south of the Mt. Paran on the Zachariah Quadrangle.

ELEVATION: 330 m (1,080 ft).

DESCRIPTION: The petroglyphs are located on a large slab of rock, which rests precariously against a ledge on the roof of the rockshelter (Fig. 89). Two sets of concentric circles are abraded into the rock surface facing toward the rockshelter opening. The circles measure 10 and 15 cm (4 and 6 in) in outer diameter (Fig. 90). Both are severely weathered and difficult to see. Some possibly cultural linear markings were also noted at one end of the boulder. Archaeological deposits in the rockshelter were dated to 310 B.C. The rockshelter did have three bedrock mortars in a separate rock.

BIBLIOGRAPHIC SOURCES: O'Steen, Gremillion, and Ledbetter 1991.

FIRST RECORDED BY AUTHORS: Coy, November 1992.

89. View of the Big Turtle Rockshelter petroglyph site.

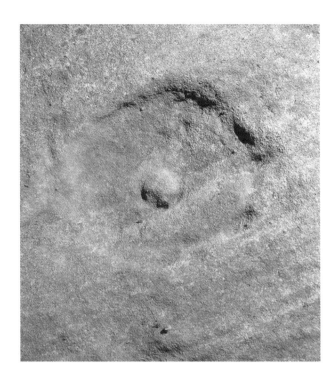

90. Concentric circle in the Big Turtle Rockshelter petroglyph site.

BIG SINKING CREEK TURTLE ROCK PETROGLYPH SITE (15LE57)

LOCATION: Lee County, northwest of Zoe, and north of Mt. Olive, on the Zachariah Quadrangle. Elevation: 320 m (1,040 ft).

DESCRIPTION: This site was first documented by G.D. Knudsen and S. Simpson, professional archaeologists for Daniel Boone National Forest, in 1982. Immediately adjacent to an oil road, the site consisted of a sandstone outcrop on a south-facing ridge north of Big Sandy Creek (Fig. 91). Bird tracks, a turtle, and historic initials were documented within an area measuring about three by four meters on the southeastern portion of the rock.

The bird tracks occur in one group of four in a straight line pointing almost due east, one group of two pointing north and southeast, and an isolated track pointing southeast (Fig. 92). Measurements of four of the bird tracks indicated that length ranged from 12–25 cm (4.8–10 in) and width ranged from 9–12 cm (3.6–4.8 in). The turtle's head pointed generally

91. View of the Big Sinking Creek Turtle Rock petroglyph site.

92. Drawing of the Big Sinking Creek Turtle Rock petroglyphs.

1 m.

93. Turtle petroglyph at Big Sinking Creek Turtle Rock.

east-southeast. It measured about 30 cm (12 in) from the tip of the head to the tail (Fig. 93).

BIBLIOGRAPHIC SOURCES: Knudsen and Simpson 1982.

FIRST RECORDED BY AUTHORS: Coy, Fuller, and Meadows, May 1971.

CAVE FORK HILL PETROGLYPH SITE (15LE110)

LOCATION: Lee County, southwest of Hopewell Church and southeast of the cemetery at Fixer, on the Zachariah Quadrangle. Elevation: about 340 m (1,120 ft).

DESCRIPTION: The site was described as follows by Funkhouser and Webb (1929, 80–82):

> Under this cliff, in sight of the road up Cave Fork Hill, is a rockshelter about thirty feet wide and forty feet deep, formed by the falling out of great stones from the vertical cliff face [Fig. 94]. This site is of interest . . . as one of the large boulders fallen from the rockshelter roof contained a good specimen of hominy hole. An unusual feature was the engraving of human footprints and bear tracks on the surface of the boulder. . . . The hominy hole in this stone is undoubtedly prehistoric; the age of these other carvings is problematical. The human tracks appear to be old and of such form as would have been familiar to the Indian or any other man not accustomed to the wearing of shoes. However, there is nothing to positively determine their age. The carving seems to have been done with a blunt-pointed chisel. It is not impossible that such result might have been accomplished by the use of flint chisels.

The present location of the boulder described by Funkhouser and Webb is unknown. It was removed and taken to the University of Kentucky campus, but attempts by Coy and Fuller failed to find the stone or anyone who knew of its whereabouts. Figure 95 illustrates the petroglyphs on this boulder. Two prints, thought to represent bear tracks, still can be seen on a large piece of roof fall centrally located in the rockshelter (Fig. 96).

BIBLIOGRAPHIC SOURCES: Funkhouser and Webb 1929.

FIRST RECORDED BY AUTHORS: Coy, August 1967.

94. View of the Cave Fork Hill petroglyph site.

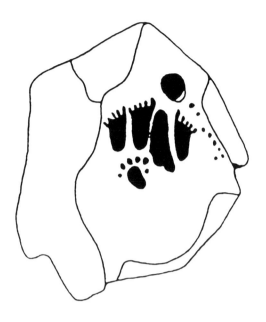

95. Drawing of human footprints and bear tracks documented by Funkhouser and Webb at Cave Fork Hill.

96. Human footprints still present at Cave Fork Hill.

PERDUE PETROGLYPH SITE (15LE111)

LOCATION: Lee County, southeast of Mt. Paran School and northwest of the cemetery at Fixer, on the Zachariah Quadrangle. Elevation: about 340 m (1,120 ft).

DESCRIPTION: This site is a sandstone rockshelter, measuring approximately 15 m (50 ft) in length and about 5 m (16 ft) in height (Fig. 97). Two petroglyphs were documented on a slab of rock that is tilted about 45° and measures about 1.5 m (5 ft) in height and 15 m (50 ft) in length (Fig. 98). The petroglyphs include a bird track and an unusual curvilinear figure that resembles an insect (Figs. 99, 100). While the bird track is a very typical example, the curvilinear figure is unique among documented Kentucky petroglyphs. It is so unusual that it is difficult to determine if it was meant to be representational or abstract. Swauger speculated that it might have been meant to represent an insect such as a dragonfly in larval form. Motifs of any of the class *Insecta* are uncommon. Motifs of the class *Arachnida* are used, especially in the western United States.

BIBLIOGRAPHIC SOURCES: None is known.

FIRST RECORDED BY AUTHORS: Coy and Fuller, August 1976.

97. View of the Perdue petroglyph site.

98. Petroglyphs at the Perdue site.

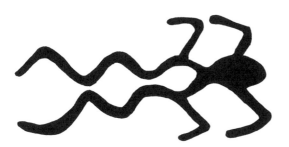

99. Drawing of Perdue petroglyphs.

100. Possible insect or larval form at Perdue.

BEAR TRACK PETROGLYPH SITE (15LE112)

LOCATION: Lee County, northeast of the Bear Track Lookout Tower and southeast of the Sandfield School, on the Cobhill Quadrangle. Elevation: about 330 m (1,080 ft).

DESCRIPTION: This site is on a sandstone outcrop at the head of Town Hollow (Fig. 101). A single petroglyph consisting of a bear track surrounded by a circle was documented (Fig. 102). The depth of the lines of the design averages from 1–1.5 cm (0.4–0.6 in). The circle, which is sharply cut, may be later than the bear paw. Many recent initials and dates are on the rock. This design is similar to those of the Daugherty Bear Track Site discussed above, but we are not at this time inclined to say that there is a relationship between them despite their obvious similarities.

BIBLIOGRAPHIC SOURCES: Fuller 1969a.

FIRST RECORDED BY AUTHORS: Coy, Fuller, and Meadows, February 1969.

101. View of the Bear Track petroglyph site.

102. Petroglyph
at Bear Track.

OLD LANDING PETROGLYPH SITE (15LE113)

LOCATION: Lee County, south of BM 646 and southwest of Sandfield School, on the Cobhill Quadrangle. Elevation: about 340 m (1,100 ft).

DESCRIPTION: The Old Landing petroglyphs are located on the south face of a cliff and consist of several series of vertical lines arranged in roughly parallel rows. Rock has spalled away considerably in at least two locations. A large cleft separates the bulk of the lines on the west side from a small cluster to the east (Figs. 103, 104).

Narrow cuts range 5–10 mm (0.20–0.39 in) in width and average 7 cm (2.8 in) in length and 5 mm (0.20 in) in depth. The wider cuts average 2 cm (0.79 in) in width, 10 cm (3.9 in) in length, and 1 cm (0.39 in) in depth. Bird tracks were also noted but are difficult to distinguish from the straight lines they accompany.

The regularity of the rows of lines at this and other similar sites has given rise to many speculations as to their meaning or function. Various researchers

103. Petroglyphs on the west side of the
panel at the Old Landing petroglyph site.

104. Petroglyphs on the east side of the
panel at the Old Landing petroglyph site.

have suggested that they represent calendrical marks, tally marks, symbols of war conquests (such as 8 "counting coup" documented for nineteenth-century North American Plains warriors) or merely served as tool sharpening sites (Swauger 1978; Murphy 1969; Weber 1971). A more unlikely speculation made by Fell (1976; 1978; 1980) is that they are records carved by early Old World explorers.

BIBLIOGRAPHIC SOURCES: None is known.

FIRST RECORDED BY AUTHORS: Coy and Meadows, October 1983.

FINCASTLE PETROGLYPH SITE (15LE120)

LOCATION: Lee County, northwest of Bethlehem Church and southwest of Fincastle Church on the Zachariah Quadrangle. Elevation: about 240 m (800 ft).

DESCRIPTION: The site is a sandstone rockshelter measuring 80 m (267 ft) at the entrance, 7 m (23 ft) in depth and 25 m (83 ft) in height. The petroglyphs are located on a boulder near the drip line (Fig. 105) and include six or seven

105. View of the Fincastle petroglyph site.

106. Bear tracks at Fincastle.

107. Drawing of animal petroglyph at Fincastle.

bear tracks and a bird track (Fig. 106). Also documented was an unusual representation that appears to be a four-footed, tailed animal with a rather long
neck and upright pointed ears. The middle of the body is transected by two
broad lines that extend beneath the belly (Fig. 107). One of the bear tracks
occurs at the top of this figure, appearing to perch on its back. A historic drill
hole left from former nitre mining operations was observed in a boulder.

The bear tracks are somewhat variable in the shape and size of the foot
pad but all show five toes. Swauger speculates that the animal figure may

have been meant to symbolize an animal or man possessed of sacred power (Swauger 1974, 50, plate 52).

BIBLIOGRAPHIC SOURCES: None is known.

FIRST RECORDED BY AUTHORS: Coy, Fuller, and Meadows, February 1973.

LITTLE SINKING PETROGLYPH SITE (15LE215)

LOCATION: Lee County, on a sandstone point overlooking Little Sinking Creek northeast of the Mt. Paran School on the Zachariah Quadrangle. Elevation: 370 m (1,200 ft).

DESCRIPTION: Severely weathered petroglyphs consisting of at least one deer track and one bird track were observed (Figs. 108, 109). Other areas may have remnants of human footprints or bear tracks.

BIBLIOGRAPHIC SOURCES: None is known.

FIRST RECORDED BY AUTHORS: Coy and Meadows, January 1972.

108. View of the Little Sinking petroglyph site.

109. View of the Little Sinking petroglyph site.

MANTLE ROCK PETROGLYPH SITE (15LV160)

LOCATION: Livingston County, south of the Cave Spring Church on the Gol-
conda Quadrangle. Elevation: 120 m (400 ft).

DESCRIPTION: Mantle Rock is a well-known historic landmark that reportedly was where the Cherokee "Trail of Tears" exited Kentucky. Several figures,
including a fish, a man, and a turkey, were pecked into a sandstone slab lay-
ing in a small rockshelter (Figs. 110, 111, 112). The petroglyphs were executed with a sharp, probably metallic tool. Although probably of historic date, the
petroglyphs may have been made by Native Americans.

BIBLIOGRAPHIC SOURCES: None is known.

FIRST RECORDED BY AUTHORS: Coy and Fuller, March 1971.

110. View of the Mantle Rock petroglyph site.

111. Human figures and turkey petroglyphs at Mantle Rock.

112. Fish petroglyph at Mantle Rock.

BURNT RIDGE PETROGLYPH SITE (15MA197)

LOCATION: Madison County, northeast of Macedonia Church on the Berea Quadrangle. Elevation: 430 m (1,400 ft).

DESCRIPTION: The petroglyphs are in a small sandstone rockshelter measuring about 9 m (30 ft) in length, 4.5 m (15 ft) in depth and 4.5 m (15 ft) in height. The rockshelter faces almost due west (Fig. 113). Three types of designs were documented. Three examples of a human stick figure were noted. One appears on a rock beyond the protection of the drip line and has almost disappeared. The stick figure illustrated in Figures 114 and 115 is on the center rock. It may be a male figure as it appears to include a penis. Alternatively, the male stick figure could be interpreted as a lizard, particularly because the appendage might have been meant by the carver to represent a short tail. The third figure is on a rock higher than the illustrated example,

113. View of the Burnt Ridge petroglyph site (Emily Coy pictured).

115. Drawing of possible human stick figure at Burnt Ridge.

114. Possible human stick figure at Burnt Ridge.

116. Raptorial bird at Burnt Ridge.

117. Drawing of raptorial bird at Burnt Ridge.

but the design was almost covered with moss at the time of survey and was not cleared by the authors, so it could not be closely examined.

The second major form is that of a raptorial bird with widespread wings (Figs. 116, 117), located on the center rock.

A third design is what can be considered chevrons carved between the bird and the stick figure. Swauger is reluctant to accept these "chevrons" as Native American. They appear too sharply cut and are unlike the obvious pit-and-groove origin of the other designs.

BIBLIOGRAPHIC SOURCES: None is known.

FIRST RECORDED BY AUTHORS: Coy and Meadows, January 1987.

PAYNEVILLE PETROGLYPH SITE (15MD308)

LOCATION: Meade County, west of Sirocco and east of Payneville on the Irvington Quadrangle. Elevation: about 220 m (720 ft).

DESCRIPTION: This site is on an outcropping of sandstone that forms a small series of ledges on a wooded hillside (Fig. 118). One area has a flat horizontal surface measuring 1.8–2.4 m (6–8 ft). Many bird tracks are carved upon this surface and surrounding stones. This site is a popular picnic spot and many historic and modern initials are superimposed upon the bird tracks (Fig. 119). There are also renderings of horseshoes and an Indian's head. The carvings

118. View of the Payneville petroglyph site.

119. Bird tracks and historic initials at Payneville.

were obscured by moss as well as superimposed initials at the time of survey, making close examination difficult (Coy and Fuller 1966, 55, fig. 9).

Despite the presence of clearly historic carvings, and other modern modifications, some of the elements, particularly the bird tracks, appear to be Native American in origin.

BIBLIOGRAPHIC SOURCES: Coy and Fuller 1966.

FIRST RECORDED BY AUTHORS: Coy and Fuller, June 1964.

INDIAN STAIRWAY PETROGLYPH SITE (15MF160)

LOCATION: Menifee County, northwest of Tower Rock and northeast of Chimney Top Rock, on the Pomeroyton Quadrangle. Elevation: about 300 m (1,000 ft).

DESCRIPTION: This site is a large sandstone rockshelter facing east (Fig. 120). It is reached by climbing the so-called Indian Stairway. Four concentric circles are carved into a sandstone slab lying on the rockshelter floor (Fig. 121).

BIBLIOGRAPHIC SOURCES: Wyss and Wyss 1977.

FIRST RECORDED BY AUTHORS: Coy and Fuller, October 1970.

120. View of the Indian Stairway petroglyph site.

121. Concentric circle petroglyphs at Indian Stairway.

STONE FOOT SHELTER PETROGLYPH SITE (15MF178)

LOCATION: Menifee County, very near the Menifee-Powell County line, north-west of Short Creek, on the Frenchburg Quadrangle. Elevation: 400 m (1,300 ft).

DESCRIPTION: The petroglyphs occur in a large east-facing rockshelter measuring 45 m (150 ft) across the front and 8 m (27 ft) in depth (Fig. 122). Dense quantities of prehistoric artifacts are associated with the shelter; bedrock mortars and a large nutting stone were noted by Jobe, et al. (1980, 66) during their investigation of the site. Diagnostic artifacts suggested a Late Archaic/Early Woodland affiliation. Evidence of severe looting in the form of potholes was observed in the rockshelter. The petroglyphs occurred on two of the many boulders in the rockshelter. One boulder containing a bedrock mortar (or hominy hole) also exhibited at least two human footprints (Fig. 123). Another rock has two or three human footprints, two deer tracks, and a geometric figure roughly resembling a figure eight (Fig. 124). The petroglyphs are severely weathered.

BIBLIOGRAPHIC SOURCES: Jobe, Stafford, and Boisvert 1980.

FIRST RECORDED BY AUTHORS: Coy, January 1994.

122. View of the Stone Foot rockshelter petroglyph site (Cecil Ison pictured).

123. View of the Stone Foot rockshelter petroglyph site.

124. View of the Stone Foot rockshelter petroglyph site (Johnny Faulkner pictured).

BELL'S FALLS PETROGLYPH SITE (15MF199)

LOCATION: Menifee County, southwest of the juncture of Powell Branch with Gladie Creek on the Pomeroyton Quadrangle. The Bell's Falls site is also known as the Upper Sal Branch Shelter. It is within the Daniel Boone National Forest. Elevation: 370 m (1,200 ft).

DESCRIPTION: The designs were pecked and ground into the sloping face of a boulder lying near the drip line of the rockshelter in which they occur (Fig. 125). A row of straight lines, and one possible and two definite split-hoof animal tracks were documented on the edge of the boulder nearest the front of the rockshelter (Fig. 126). A bird track and other less clear marks are pecked on the wall in the rear of the boulder.

Gary D. Knudsen recorded this site in 1980 as the Upper Sal Branch Rockshelter. Primarily because of the petroglyph, he recommended that it be included in the Forest Service's Multiple Resource District nomination and be considered eligible for the National Register of Historic Places.

BIBLIOGRAPHIC SOURCES: Knudsen 1980.

FIRST RECORDED BY AUTHORS: Coy and Meadows, June 1976.

125. View of the Bell's Falls petroglyph site.

126. Petroglyphs at Bell's Falls.

SPRATT'S PETROGLYPH SITE (15MF353)

LOCATION: Menifee County, southeast of Natural Arch and northwest of Kendrick Ridge Church, on the Scranton Quadrangle. Elevation: about 340 m (1,100 ft).

DESCRIPTION: The carvings were documented in an east-facing sandstone rockshelter having only a shallow overhang (Fig. 127). The petroglyphs are

127. View of Spratt's petroglyph site (Dr. Fred Coy III pictured).

128. Petroglyphs at Spratt's.

located on a boulder situated in the north-central portion of the rockshelter. The boulder measures 1.8 by 1.7 m (6 by 5.7 ft). The design elements are arranged in a linear fashion across the upper face of the boulder, along with some extraneous elements on the same rock face. The main group of elements include abstract and curvilinear designs with at least two bird tracks (Fig. 128). The extraneous elements consist of one bird track south of the main line of elements and one possible paw print north and west of the main group.

BIBLIOGRAPHIC SOURCES: None is known.

FIRST RECORDED BY AUTHORS: Coy, Fuller, and Meadows, November 1974.

SKIDMORE PETROGLYPH SITE (15MF354)

LOCATION: The Skidmore Petroglyph Site is in Menifee County, south of Hawkins Branch School and southwest of Leatherwood School, on the French-burg Quadrangle. It is also known as the Short Creek Site. Elevation: 420 m (1,380 ft).

DESCRIPTION: The petroglyphs appear on boulders in a large, south-facing rockshelter, measuring 30 m (98 ft) in width and 7.4–8.5 m (24.6–28.3 ft) in

129. View of the Skidmore petroglyph
site. (Photo by Ernest M. Ellison.)

depth (Fig. 129). Two large boulders near the central portion of the rockshelter contain the main group of petroglyphs (Fig. 130). Coy and Fuller (1971)
described the markings as "the most irregular, confused group of carvings we
have yet run into." It has been suggested that the multiple-branched,
pecked-out petroglyph with terminal clusters in the upper portion of the panel
may represent a plant. Plant motifs are very unusual in Eastern United
States rock art. Several bird tracks lacking hind toes (Fig. 131) were identified
but the other marks were difficult to identify with a descriptive term. Other
clearer bird tracks were noted on another rock. Several small bedrock mortars
are found in rocks separate from the one containing the petroglyphs.

BIBLIOGRAPHIC SOURCES: Coy and Fuller 1971.

FIRST RECORDED BY AUTHORS: Coy, Fuller, and Meadows, November 1971.

130. The Skidmore petroglyphs.

131. Drawing of Skidmore petroglyphs.

MARTIN FORK PETROGLYPH SITE (15PO23)

LOCATION: Powell County, south of the juncture of Martin Fork and Grays Branch of the Red River and south of the juncture of Dunkard's Branch and the Red River, on the Slade Quadrangle. Elevation: about 350 m (1,150 ft).

DESCRIPTION: The petroglyphs are on two boulders in a large sandstone rockshelter situated in a roughly semicircular cliff face, easily seen from a distance (Fig. 132). The Martin Fork headwaters begin 50 m (167 ft) below this rockshelter. Coy and Fuller (1971, 117–20, figs. 86–88) described the rockshelter as measuring 60 m (200 ft) in length, 18 m (60 ft) in height, 12 m (40 ft) in depth, and facing 270 degrees. It is dry in the upper parts of the rockshelter; however, a small stream flows over a waterfall at the south end, and this area is damp. The rockshelter has been dug extensively by people hunting artifacts.

A large sandstone boulder, measuring 1.5 m by 1.2 m by 90 cm (5 ft by 4 ft by 3 ft), on which most of the petroglyphs occur is well within the protected

132. View of the Martin Fork petroglyph site.

133. Elk tracks at Martin Fork.

limits of the rockshelter (Fig. 133). The carvings include at least three sets of large hoof tracks interpreted as "elk tracks" rather than deer. Two rings forming a concentric circle, an "elk track" and other indistinct carvings are observable at the north end of the boulder (Fig. 134). The south end of the rock contains a nearly obliterated carving that appears to be a large bird track. All of the petroglyphs were made by initially pecking the design followed by smoothing and abrasion. Another boulder three meters northwest of the large boulder exhibited two cloven hoof tracks, one of which is much larger than typical deer tracks (Fig. 135).

Because of the damage the petroglyphs have sustained from frequent visits by hikers, relic collectors, and others, the U.S. Forest Service, which owns the site, has placed a fence around the petroglyphs to prevent further damage.

BIBLIOGRAPHIC SOURCES: Coy and Fuller 1971; Weinland and Sanders 1977.

FIRST RECORDED BY AUTHORS: Coy, Fuller, and Meadows, May 1970.

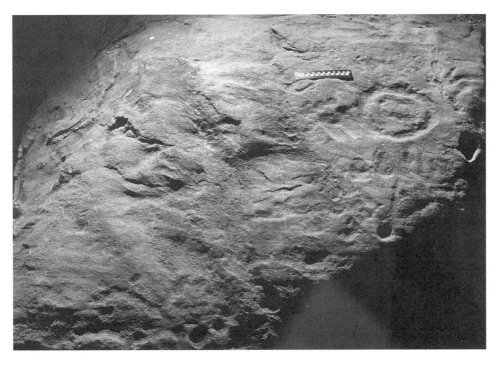

134. Concentric circle and other petroglyphs at Martin Fork.

135. Atypically large cloven
hoof tracks at Martin Fork.

HIGH ROCK PETROGLYPH SITE (15PO25)

LOCATION: Powell County, north of Rogers Chapel and southeast of Cat Creek Church, on the Stanton Quadrangle. Elevation: about 410 m (1350 ft).

DESCRIPTION: The High Rock petroglyphs are in a sandstone rockshelter, measuring 47 m (157 ft) in length, 9.6 m (32 ft) in depth, 15–18 m (50–60 ft) in height and facing south by southwest. There are other rockshelters and cliffs along this general formation. All of the rockshelters, including the one containing petroglyphs, have been impacted by nonprofessional digging to collect prehistoric artifacts.

The petroglyphs appear on a sandstone boulder, measuring about 1.5 by 0.6 by 1.2 m (5 ft by 2 ft by 4 ft) in the opening of the rockshelter (Fig. 136). On the front face of this rock, in an area measuring 0.6 by 1.5 m (2 by 5 ft), is a sophisticated group of carvings produced primarily by pecking, but with some smoothing by abrasion. The carvings include a complex series of geometric and linear designs covering one side of the boulder (Fig. 137). Two smooth areas on the rear of the rock contain small shallow markings that may represent unfinished attempts. This rock was moved for its protection and now is housed in the Red River Museum in Clay City.

The deep reaches of this rockshelter remain dry; however, at times considerable water falls from the cliff above the rockshelter. Despite considerable

136. View of the High Rock petroglyph site.

137. Complex geometric motifs at High Rock.

"pot hunting" in this rockshelter, the petroglyphs are not particularly vandalized and only fragmented somewhat around the periphery due to the friable sandstone on which they occur. Thus the outer margins have been lost (Coy and Fuller 1971: 114–19).

The elaborate set of designs at the site is most unusual. Swauger (1974, 48–50; plates 51, 53) documented a design (no. 7) at the Parkers Landing Site (36CL1) in Pennsylvania that he characterized as having a Central American flair; his reaction to the High Rock geometric and linear petroglyphs is similar. While he does not think these designs are proof of any association between Kentucky and Central America or between the site in Kentucky and the one in Pennsylvania, he does feel that the High Rock petroglyphs are complicated beyond the normal designs found in the northeastern United States. It is most unlikely that the two designs of the site were created by the same petroglyph artist, and it is probable that they were not created at the same time although, considering the discrepancies in expertise normal among groups of human beings, we cannot say they were not contemporary with each other. The rock with the petroglyphs contains bedrock mortars, which have been enhanced within recent years.

BIBLIOGRAPHIC SOURCES: Coy and Fuller 1971; Weinland and Sanders 1977.

FIRST RECORDED BY AUTHORS: Coy, Fuller, and Meadows, May 1970.

STATE ROCK PETROGLYPH SITE (15PO106)

LOCATION: Powell County, at State Rock, which is prominently marked on the Stanton Quadrangle. Elevation: about 390 m (1,280 ft).

DESCRIPTION: This site was first documented by Weinland and Sanders (1977), who noted the presence of three-toed "turkey tracks" and some historic

138. View of the State Rock petroglyph site.

139. Petroglyphs at State Rock.

initials. These tracks occur at the top of naturally formed steps near the highest level of State Rock (Fig. 138) and include two tracks that definitely appeared to be Native American in origin and one possible track now obscured by a superimposed "V" initial of questionable age (Fig. 139).

BIBLIOGRAPHIC SOURCES: Weinland and Sanders 1977.

FIRST RECORDED BY AUTHORS: Coy, Fuller, and Meadows, January 1973.

MCKINNEY BLUFF PETROGLYPH SITE (15PO107)

LOCATION: Powell County, southwest of the juncture of Short Creek and Red River and northwest of Middle Fork Church, on the Slade Quadrangle. Elevation: about 330 m (1,080 ft).

DESCRIPTION: Weinland and Sanders documented this site in 1977. The petroglyphs are in a rockshelter on the east slope of McKinney Cliff (Fig. 140),

140. View of the McKinney Bluffs petroglyph site.

141. Pair of human footprint petroglyphs at McKinney Bluff.

and are represented by four human-like footprints, carved on a large boulder, measuring 1.2 by 1.4 m (3.4 by 4.6 ft). The footprints are equivalent in size, measuring 14 cm (5.6 in) in length and 5 cm (2 in) in width. One pair is close together and perpendicular (Fig. 141).

BIBLIOGRAPHIC SOURCES: Weinland and Sanders 1977.

FIRST RECORDED BY AUTHORS: Coy, Fuller, and Meadows, March 1973.

AMBURGY HOLLOW PETROGLYPH SITE (15PO108)

LOCATION: Powell County, northwest of Courthouse Rock and east of the juncture of Spaas Creek and the Red River, on the Slade Quadrangle. Elevation: about 340 m (1,100 ft).

142. View of the Amburgy
Hollow petroglyph site.

DESCRIPTION: This site was first documented by Coy and Fuller in 1971
and was later revisited by Weinland and Sanders (1977). The petroglyphs
are in a sandstone rockshelter, measuring 10.4 m (34.3 ft) in width, 7.6 m
(25 ft) in depth and 4 m (13.2 ft) in height. Observable designs include a
series of cut lines similar to those at the Old Landing Site (15LE113) and
Red Bird River (15CY51). These are located on the southeast wall, con-
fined to an area of 1.2 to 1.5 m (4–5 ft) (Fig. 143). Meadows reported that
there had once been deer tracks and other designs on the rear wall, but
they are now gone, apparently destroyed when someone tried to remove
them (Fig. 144).

BIBLIOGRAPHIC SOURCES: Coy and Fuller 1971; Weinland and Sanders 1977.

FIRST RECORDED BY AUTHORS: Coy, Fuller, and Meadows, May 1970.

143. Petroglyphs at Amburgy Hollow.

144. Rear wall at Amburgy Hollow showing destruction of petroglyphs.

WHITE'S PETROGLYPH SITE (15PO154)

LOCATION: Powell County, near the Estill County line, southwest of Rogers Chapel and east of State Rock, on the Stanton Quadrangle. The site is also known as Faye's Petroglyph Site. Elevation: 340 m (1,100 ft).

DESCRIPTION: This site is an east-facing sandstone rockshelter (Fig. 145) containing a large boulder 1.4 m (4.6 ft) in length, 1 m (3.3 ft) in height, and 32 cm (12.8 in) in thickness bearing a group of designs. These petroglyphs include circular and wavy line elements that were pounded and rubbed into the surface facing toward the interior of the rockshelter (Fig. 146). A second design, identified as a chevron, is on a ledge 2 m (6.6 ft) north of the main boulder (Fig. 147).

BIBLIOGRAPHIC SOURCES: None is known.

FIRST RECORDED BY AUTHORS: Coy, Fuller, and Meadows, August 1972.

145. View of White's petroglyph site.

146. Circular and wavy line petroglyphs at White's.

NADA TUNNEL 1 PETROGLYPH SITE (15PO155)

LOCATION: Powell County, southwest of the juncture of Schoolhouse Branch and the Red River on the Slade Quadrangle. Elevation: 300 m (1000 ft).

DESCRIPTION: The petroglyphs are in a shallow cave, 3 m (10 ft) wide at the mouth, a maximum of 2 m (6.6 ft) in depth, and 1.1 m (3.6 ft) in maximum height (Fig. 147). The designs were inscribed on the rear wall, and consist of narrow lines forming a series of "V" shapes (Fig. 148). One set of lines is enclosed and forms a triangular element. The carvings measure about 31 cm (12.4 in) north to south on the east wall at a height of about 21 cm (8.4 in). The lines average about 6 mm (0.2 in) in depth.

Some may question the assignment of this site to the Native American group. While similar to lines suggested to be the result of tool sharpening, the lines in this site are thinner, have a sharper cross section and appear to form a purposeful pattern, rather than the relatively patternless lines at such sites as Amburgy Hollow, Old Landing, or Red Bird River. Swauger believes that the designs once formed three chevrons but that the center chevron has erod-ed. It may be significant that the "chevron" patterns here are generally simi-

147. View of the Nada Tunnel 1 petroglyph site.

148. Petroglyphs at Nada Tunnel 1.

lar although not identical to those noted in the White's Petroglyph Site (15PO154), located only 7.5 miles away.

BIBLIOGRAPHIC SOURCES: None is known.

FIRST RECORDED BY AUTHORS: Coy, January 1973.

NADA TUNNEL 2 PETROGLYPH SITE (15PO156)

LOCATION: Powell County, southwest of the juncture of Schoolhouse Branch and Red River on the Slade Quadrangle. Elevation: about 370 m (1,220 ft).

DESCRIPTION: The petroglyphs are in a large, northwest-facing sandstone rockshelter at the head of Moreland Branch (Fig. 149). Three elements forming concentric circles identified as Native American manufacture are on a north-slanting rock facing outward from the back wall of the rockshelter (Fig. 150). The rock also contains numerous modern petroglyphs (mostly initials).

Concentric circles have been documented at several other sites including Tar Springs (15BC129), Pilot Rock (15CH200), Martin Fork (15PO23), and White's (15PO154).

BIBLIOGRAPHIC SOURCES: None is known.

FIRST RECORDED BY AUTHORS: Coy and Fuller, August 1976.

149. View of the Nada Tunnel 2 petroglyph site.

150. Circular petroglyphs at Nada Tunnel 2.

BRANHAM RIDGE PETROGLYPH SITE (15PO158)

LOCATION: Powell County, southeast of Vaughns Mill and east of the juncture of Kueshner Branch and Little Hardwicke Creek, on the Clay City Quadrangle. The site is also known as Buckner Ridge and Hardwicke Branch. Elevation: 400 m (1,300 ft).

DESCRIPTION: The petroglyphs are carved into a sandstone outcrop on top of the ridge (Fig. 151). Numerous bird tracks are observable on the rock. They are oriented in all directions (Fig. 152).

BIBLIOGRAPHIC SOURCES: None is known.

FIRST RECORDED BY AUTHORS: Coy, Fuller, and Meadows, February 1971.

151. View of the Branham Ridge petroglyph site.

152. Bird tracks at Branham Ridge.

KNOX PETROGLYPH SITE (15PO159)

LOCATION: Powell County, southeast of Cat Creek Church and east of State Rock, on the Stanton Quadrangle. Elevation: 346 m (1,135 ft).

DESCRIPTION: The petroglyphs are in a small cave, 3 m (10 ft) in width and 10 m (33 ft) in depth, facing north above the South Fork of the Red River (Fig. 153). The designs include five bird and two cloven hoof tracks carved on a 30 by 40 cm (12 by 16 in) panel on the west wall of the cave (Figure 154).

BIBLIOGRAPHIC SOURCES: None is known.

FIRST RECORDED BY AUTHORS: Coy and Meadows, July 1977.

153. View of the Knox petroglyph site.

154. Petroglyphs at Knox.

STEVEN DEHART PETROGLYPH SITE (15PO160)

LOCATION: Powell County, north of the Slade Interchange and east of Middle Fork Church, on the Slade Quadrangle. Elevation:about 300 m (1000 ft).

DESCRIPTION: The petroglyphs are located on a boulder in a small rockshelter near the DeHart Rockshelter, first recorded by Funkhouser and Webb (1930; 1932). The rockshelter faces southwest and is small in size, measuring only 14 m (46.2 ft) in width, 5 m (16.5 ft) in depth, and 3–5 m (10–16.5 ft) in height (Fig. 155). The petroglyphs are located on a block of roof fall in the northwest half of the rockshelter (Fig. 156). The carvings include linear elements interpreted as abrading lines and paw marks.

Funkhouser and Webb (1930, 283–94) described the assemblage from the DeHart Rockshelter as including ceramics in the upper levels as well as extensive "ash beds" without ceramics. Corn cobs, shell spoons, and gourd fragments were also recovered from various hearth features. These artifacts suggest Woodland or late prehistoric components; however, the rockshelter may also have earlier deposits. Insufficient contextual evidence is available to associate the petroglyphs with the cultural deposits.

BIBLIOGRAPHIC SOURCES: Funkhouser and Webb 1930, 283–85, fig. 38; 1932, 343, fig. 48.

FIRST RECORDED BY AUTHORS: Coy, Fuller, and Meadows, March 1971.

155. View of the Steven DeHart petroglyph site.

156. Petroglyphs at Steven DeHart.

LEDFORD HOLLOW PETROGLYPH SITE (15PO281)

LOCATION: Powell County, northeast of the Slade Interchange on the Mountain Parkway and southeast of the Moreland Branch Church, on the Slade Quadrangle. Elevation: about 360 m (1,170 ft).

157. View of the Ledford Hollow petroglyph site.

158. Human footprint petroglyphs at Ledford Hollow.

DESCRIPTION: The petroglyphs are in a south facing rockshelter measuring 23.8 m (78.5 ft) in width, 20 m (66 ft) in height, and 17 m (56 ft) in depth (Fig. 157). Two well-executed human footprints were pecked and abraded in a stone near the front of the rockshelter (Fig. 158). The prints are unusual in that both have only four toes and well-defined arches.

BIBLIOGRAPHIC SOURCES: None is known.

FIRST RECORDED BY AUTHORS: Coy, May 1989.

LOMAN HILL PETROGLYPH SITE (15RK49)

LOCATION: Rockcastle County, south of Dicycope Chapel and northwest of Climax Church, on the Johnetta Quadrangle. It was first registered as Loman Branch by Carnegie Museum. Elevation: 440 m (1,440 ft).

DESCRIPTION: The petroglyphs associated with this site were carved into a sandstone ledge outcropping on top of a ridge (Fig. 159). Dr. Wilbur G. Burroughs, a geologist at Berea College, first documented "a series of 12 foot-prints shaped strangely like those of human feet" (Burroughs 1938a,

159. View of the Loman Hill petroglyph site.

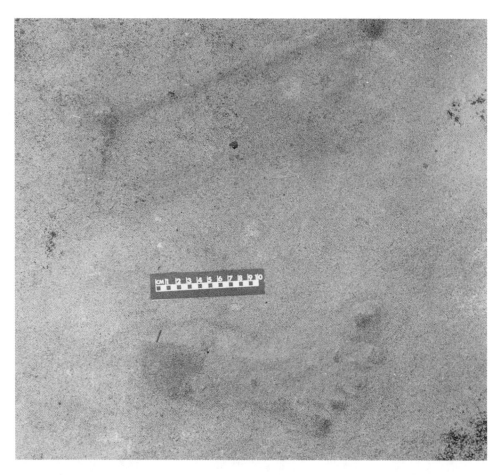

160. Toed footprints at Loman Hill.

161. Footprint without toes at Loman Hill.

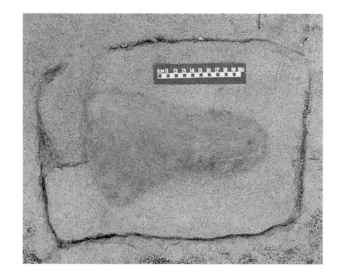

162. Destroyed petroglyphs at Loman Hill.

1938b, and 1940). Burroughs was convinced that the prints were made "by actual animal feet, back in Coal Age days when the stuff that is now stone was soft wet sand." David I. Bushnell, Jr., an eminent ethnologist with the Smithsonian Institution, strongly disagreed with this interpretation, saying "every print he examined was undoubtedly an Indian carving." Swauger, Coy, and Fuller recorded five toed prints, one or two prints without toes, and an arrow (Figs. 160, 161). Between 1970 and 1972, the petroglyphs were completely destroyed by someone trying to remove them (Fig. 162).

Despite Burroughs's conviction that these petroglyphs were 250 million years old, we believe the designs are the ordinary results of Native American artistic effort as found on other sites we have recorded in Kentucky.

BIBLIOGRAPHIC SOURCES: Coy 1991, 1993.

FIRST RECORDED BY AUTHORS: Coy and Fuller, August 1970.

JABEZ PETROGLYPH SITE (15RU42)

LOCATION: Russell County, southeast of Lake View Church and north of Coleman Church, on the Jabez Quadrangle. Elevation: about 300 m (980 ft).

163. View of the Jabez petroglyph site.

DESCRIPTION: The designs include a series of eight human footprints on the north wall of a narrow cave or rockshelter near the top of a bluff overlooking the Cumberland River and Cumberland Lake (Fig. 163). The number of toes vary from three to five. It is possible that two or more designs were once present just to the right of the highest foot shown in Figures 164 and 165, but they are not clear. An additional ten similar footprints are observable outside the cave on a wall section exposed to the weather.

BIBLIOGRAPHIC SOURCES: None is known.

FIRST RECORDED BY AUTHORS: Coy and Fuller, June 1974.

164. Petroglyphs at Jabez.

165. Drawing of the petroglyphs at Jabez.

CAESAR HURST ROCKSHELTER PETROGLYPH SITE (15WO19)

LOCATION: Wolfe County, southwest of Grannis and east of Big Andy Church, on the Campton Quadrangle. Elevation: about 310 m (1,020 ft).

DESCRIPTION: This site was first documented in 1931 by Drs. C.N. Kavanaugh and E. S. Maxwell, who sent their findings to Drs. William S. Webb and William D. Funkhouser at the University of Kentucky. Funkhouser and Webb included the site in their 1932 survey report of Kentucky archaeological sites. The rockshelter is 60 m (200 ft) in width, 18 m (60 ft) in depth, and at least 21 m (70 ft) in height (Fig. 166). Kavanaugh and Maxwell reported that a large boulder in the west area of the rockshelter contained two bird tracks and an arrow pointing toward the rockshelter (Funkhouser and Webb 1932, 411). Revisits to the site documented four turkey tracks and a bow and arrow on a large boulder in the west end of the rockshelter (Fig. 167). A hominy hole was also recorded on a nearby boulder.

Assuming that the 1931 report was accurate in its listing of the types and frequencies of designs, this site appears to have been modified and added to by modern non–Native American carvers. While the arrow may be of genuine Native American manufacture, the bow is considered a later addition.

BIBLIOGRAPHIC SOURCES: Funkhouser and Webb 1932.

FIRST RECORDED BY AUTHORS: Coy and Meadows, July 1972.

166. View of the Caesar Hurst petroglyph site.

167. Petroglyphs at Caesar Hurst (deer track and bow on boulder at top of figure).

TRINITY SHELTER PETROGLYPH SITE (15WO26)

LOCATION: Wolfe County, south of Tower Rock on the Pomeroyton Quadrangle. Elevation: about 310 m (1,020 ft).

DESCRIPTION: This site is the central rockshelter in a series of three connected rockshelters situated in a gently curving sandstone formation. The rockshelters' boundaries are not particularly sharp although the rockshelter to the east is more set apart from the one with the petroglyphs than is the rockshelter to the west. Trinity Rockshelter is 50 m (165 ft) deep and of equal width at the drip line. The designs are carved into a boulder lying about 22 m (72.6 ft) from the southern end of the drip line and about halfway between the drip line and the back wall of the rockshelter. The boulder is 91 cm (36.4 in) long and 48 cm (19.2 in) wide (Fig. 168). Identifiable petroglyphs include a footprint near the northern arc of the boulder, a possible vulva form just to the south of the footprint, a possible human stick figure touching the vulva form on the west, and a series of V-shaped elements that may be animal tracks, possibly deer (Fig. 169).

168. View of the Trinity
Rockshelter petroglyph site.

169. Petroglyphs at Trinity
Rockshelter.

In addition to the "V"-shaped designs that may have been meant to be animal tracks of some sort, on the eastern arc of the rock there is what may have
been meant to be a deer track, two lines bearing slightly south of west. Slightly west of north of these possible deer tracks is what may have been meant to

be a human figure with its left arm (as one faces the boulder) apparently waving some sort of curved device.

It may also be true that the waving figure is not a single design after all, but that the presumed association with the broad "U" to the northwest is not a true association but an accident of sculpturing, and that what seem like legs produced by the "U" is instead a vulva design such as found on the Sparks Indian Rock House Petroglyph Site. The foot along the northern edge of the boulder is believed to be a representation of a human foot.

BIBLIOGRAPHIC SOURCES: None is known.

FIRST RECORDED BY AUTHORS: Coy, November 1973.

SEVENTEEN SEVENTEEN PETROGLYPH SITE (15WO119)

LOCATION: Wolfe County, northeast of the juncture of Lower Devil Creek and Panther Branch and northwest of Grannie, on the Campton Quadrangle. Its elevation is approximately 300 m (1,000 ft).

DESCRIPTION: The petroglyphs are incised on a sandstone outcrop (Fig. 170) at the base of a cliff line. Five or six bird tracks were recorded in two sections (Fig. 171). A historic carving of "1717" was also noted (Fig. 172). While this

170. View of the 1717 petroglyph site.

171. Bird tracks at 1717.

172. 1717 petroglyph at 1717.

may be a date, it is considerably earlier than that of the first documented visit of a Euro-American to Kentucky, that of Dr. Thomas Walker in 1750.

BIBLIOGRAPHIC SOURCES: None is known.

FIRST RECORDED BY AUTHORS: Coy, Fuller, and Meadows, July 1972.

3

DESTROYED OR
QUESTIONABLE SITES

WICKLIFFE PETROGLYPH SITE (15BA109)

LOCATION: Ballard County, reportedly in a red sandstone bed on Cane Creek, north of Cane Creek Church and west northwest of Harrison Hughes Cemetery on the Wickliffe Quadrangle. It was just downstream from the bridge over Cane Creek. Elevation: about 110 m (350 ft).

DESCRIPTION: The only available information for this site is a written description from the late nineteenth century. R.H. Loughridge published a detailed description and an illustration of the petroglyphs (Fig. 173) in 1888. It is reprinted in its entirety here:

> Foot-prints in Sandstone. A locality of very special interest occurs a couple of miles northeast of Wickliffe, in the bed of a small branch emptying into Cane creek from the north, and on the place of Mrs. R. Burns. In the bed of this branch is a broad sandstone, reddish in color, its surface somewhat uneven from the action of water running over it, and covering an extent of about twenty feet in length. In its width it is exposed for only about six feet, being covered in the valley to the west by the washings from the hillside.

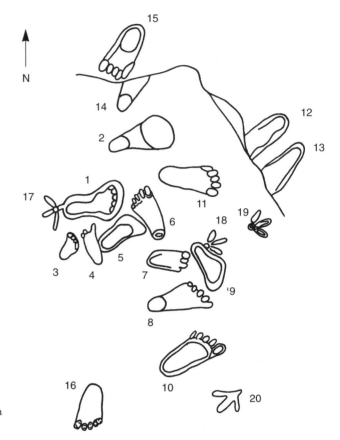

173. Loughridge's illustration
of the Wickliffe petroglyphs.

The hills rise about forty feet above this rock, and are formed of Quaternary silt, loam and gravel—the rock disappearing beneath them. Upon the surface of the sandstone are easily traced human foot-prints and large bird tracks, in some cases deeply indented one-half inch, with the conformation of the bottom of the foot and toes; in others but shallow imprints, one-eighth of an inch deep, in which the toes do not appear, and in which there is lacking the barefoot feature, indicating rather a moccasined foot. The tracks are in every direction and position, the stream flowing across them in a northward course.

A peculiarity of the imprints is in the fact that all but three are of the left foot.

In some cases the toes are deeply indented, while the rest of the sole of the foot is shallow; sometimes the space between the toes is filled.

A sketch showing the position and size of each foot was made by means of tracing linen and pencil; and is given below in a form reduced by photography. The outer lines mark the extreme limits, while the interior lines indicate the deepest portion of the track.

The rock is several feet thick, reaches across the branch and into the opposite bank on the east. Upon the latter portion a large bird track was seen, and also what seems to be a part of a human foot-print.

The following are the measurements and peculiarities of each track, as numbered in the accompanying photographic print.

No. 1. Right foot. Central impression deep, with sloping sides and showing a clear outline of the instep. The toe impressions are very faint, and only in the lowest depression, and sink a little below its surface. Extreme length, 11 3/4 inches; spread of toes, 5 3/4 inches. The foot was apparently moccasined, the toes having nearly worn through. The outer line shows the edge of the moccasin.

No. 2. Left foot, the probable mate of No. 1. The toes not so apparent, but still discernible. Instep shallow; heel and ball of foot deeper, as indicated in the sketch. Also covered by a moccasin. Extreme length, 11 1/2 inches; heel, 2 1/2 inches; and spread of toes, 6 inches.

No. 3. Right foot of a child. Deep impression of foot and toes; that of the two smallest toes combined. Length, 4 1/2 inches; heel, 2 inches; toes, 3 inches.

No. 4. Left foot highly deformed. Impression distinct; big toe projected; second and third absent in imprint. Length, 7 inches; heel, 2 inches; toes, 3 1/2 inches, the balls sinking deeply.

No. 5. Left foot, probably with moccasin; deep impression, with no toes; sloping inward on all sides to the inner depression. Length, 9 inches; heel, 3 inches; toes, 4 1/4 inches.

No. 6. Left foot, with irregular toe impressions. The heel deeply, and the rest of the foot shallowly impressed, except the big toe, which sinks deeply. Length, 9 inches; heel, 2 1/2 inches; toes, 4 1/2 inches; spaces between the toes but slightly raised.

No. 7. Right foot; very broad, but shallow impression, deepest near the heel; toes run together. Length, 7 1/2 inches; heel and toes, each, 3 1/2 inches.

No. 8. Left foot; shallow impression, but deeper heel; the toes distinct, but imprints widely separated, and the sand filling the intervening spaces apparently removed. Length, 11 inches; heel, 2 1/2 inches; toes, 6 inches.

No. 9. Left foot, with moccasin. Impression shallow, with slope from outer to inner line; foot broad, but heel very narrow. Length, 8 1/2 inches; heel, 2 1/4 inches; toes, 5 inches.

No. 10. Left foot, deep impression, sloping upward at edges; toes widely separated, and not very distinct, except the largest; sand between toes not removed; no instep. Extreme length, 12 inches; heel, 3 1/4 inches; toes, 6 1/2 inches. Inside length, 8 1/2 inches; heel, 2 1/4 inches; toes, 4 inches. Big toe, outside length, 2 1/4 inches; width, 1 3/4 inches. Big toe, inside length, 1 3/8 inches; width, 1 1/4 inches.

No. 11. Shallow impression, but toes deeply impressed. Length, 10 1/4 inches; heel, 3 inches; toes, 5 1/2 inches; big toe, 2 by 1/2 inches.

Nos. 12 and 13. Shallow impression; heels a little deeper; toes apparently hid beneath the thin ledge on which are the other footprints.

No. 14. Right foot; shallow impression, but heel a little deeper; toe imprints either lost by the breaking off of the rock, or by the foot reaching beyond the edge. It lies a little above No. 15.

No. 15. Left foot; shallow impression, but heels and toes deeper. It is upon the lower surface with 12 and 13, and below the large body of foot-prints. Length, 10 1/2 inches; width of heel, 3 inches; toes, 5 1/4 inches; big toe, 2 by 1 1/2 inches.

No. 16. Left foot; shallow impression of the foot, but the toes deeply depressed. Length of foot, 9 inches; spread of toes, 6 inches; width of heel, 3 inches.

No. 17. Bird track; deep impression; the back toe overlapping the foot imprint No. 1. Spread of toes, 5 1/2 inches; length of toes, 3 inches.

No. 18. Bird track. Spread of toes, 4 1/4 inches; length of toes, 4 1/2 inches.

No. 19. Bird track; deep impression; back toe absent. Spread of toes, 4 1/2 inches; center toe, 3 1/2 inches, and side toes, 3 inches long.

No. 20. Bird track; only three toes appear. Spread, 5 1/2 inches; length of middle toe, 5 1/2 inches; side toes, 5 and 4 inches.

The foot-prints seem to be naturally formed by the direct imprint of the feet in the slightly yielding Quaternary sand, before the latter was hardened into a rock by the permeation of iron oxide, the cementing material. These sandstones are, in other localities, even in this day, in process of formation, wherever the sands and gravel of the Quaternary gravel-beds are exposed to the action of the weather. A very great antiquity, therefore, can not be claimed for these tracks<m->at least, not more remote than the mound-builders, or Indians, whose mounds and earthworks are found upon the Mississippi river bluffs, a mile or more to westward.

In all the above footprints there is an entire absence of anything like the mark of an implement that could be used in chiseling them into shape. (Loughridge 1888, 187–91, 1 fig.)

David I. Bushnell Jr. mentioned the Wickliffe Petroglyph Site in a 1913 study of human feet imprints. He apparently did not visit the site, merely reporting that "several examples of 'footprints' occur on the surface of a mass of red sandstone about three miles northeast of Wickliffe, Ballard County, Kentucky, at a point near the mouth of the Ohio. One is said to measure 12 inches in length, another 8 inches" (Bushnell 1913, 10).

Tom Fuller has visited the area on at least two occasions and found an iron-cemented sand rime forming around small branches of weeds and bushes exposed to water of the creek. He has at the present time an example of this phenomenom at his home.

BIBLIOGRAPHIC SOURCES: Coy 1991, 1993; Bushnell 1913; Fuller 1985; Loughridge 1888.

CATLETTSBURG PETROGLYPH SITE (15BD81)

LOCATION: Boyd County, first described by Squier and Davis (1848, 248), who located it at the juncture of the Big Sandy and Ohio Rivers at Catlettsburg. This information enables us to place the site northeast of the Second Ward School and north northeast of the England Hill School, on the Catlettsburg Quadrangle. Elevation: about 150 m (500 ft).

DESCRIPTION: Squier and Davis (1848, 298) recorded that the site had been destroyed "by a Vandal, to furnish the materials for building a chimney and walling a cellar" about two years before they wrote about it. They were unable to procure a specific description of its petroglyphs, reporting merely that "it is represented to have been charged with numerous outline figures and emblematic devices" (1848, 298–99).

BIBLIOGRAPHIC SOURCES: Coy 1991, 1993; Squire and Davis, 1848.

PORTSMOUTH INDIAN HEAD PETROGLYPH SITE (15GP173)

LOCATION: Greenup County; Collins (1874, vol. 1:73) states, "In Greenup County, opposite Portsmouth, Ohio, is a water-mark called the 'Indian Head,' a human face rudely carved by the aborigines, many years ago, upon the eastern side of a large rock embedded in the water of the Ohio river."

DESCRIPTION: The damming of the Ohio River for navigational purposes and flood control raised the water level so that the rock on which the petroglyph is carved is permanently under water. However, we have in our possession a copy of a photograph taken when the rock was only partly submerged. We are told that the rock is located on the Kentucky side of the Ohio River upstream from the foot of the bridge halfway to the old ferry landing.

BIBLIOGRAPHIC SOURCES: Collins 1874; Coy 1991, 1993.

GRAYSON SPRINGS PETROGLYPH SITE (NO SITE NUMBER)

LOCATION: Grayson County; Collins (1874, 2:4) reported this site to be near Grayson Springs, which is on the Clarkson Quadrangle. Local information reports that the petroglyphs were along the face of the cliff immediately west of Grayson Springs.

DESCRIPTION: According to Collins: "In the solid limestone rock . . . are the exact and perfect tracks of human feet, much larger than the ordinary size; the toes, heels, length and breadth of the feet are imprinted with wonderful exactness" (1874, 2:4).

While the presence of well-sculptured human footprints is not an anomaly in the region, their reported occurrence in limestone is unusual. However, as this site was not located, we are unable to confirm that the reported petroglyphs were genuine.

BIBLIOGRAPHIC SOURCES: Collins 1874; Coy 1991, 1993.

PINE KNOB PETROGLYPH SITE (15GY68)

LOCATION: Grayson County, in a rockshelter north of Walnut Grove Church on the Spring Lick Quadrangle. Elevation: 210 m (700 ft).

DESCRIPTION: This site is believed to be the place once inhabited by Dock Brown, an outlaw whose biography was written by William R. Haynes (1876, 4). Haynes described the Pine Knob Site as follows: "The cliff-sides are full of caverns, from stock-shelter below to eagles' eyries and ravens' nests above. In the floors of the cave [presumably the Pine Knob Shelter] are Indian mortars in which the aborigines pounded out their maize. There are also horses, mule, sheep, deer and bird tracks in the solid rock, as plainly visible as though newly made in the plastic clay."

The Pine Knob rockshelter is now a picnic spot. Whatever evidence of petroglyphs there may have been in the rockshelter is now lacking. While reports by Haynes and Collins support the supposition that petroglyphs once existed here, they cannot be adequately evaluated on present evidence.

BIBLIOGRAPHIC SOURCES: Coy 1991, 1993; Haynes 1876.

CLOVER BOTTOM PETROGLYPH SITE (15JA162)

LOCATION: Jackson County; first reported by W.E. Barton of Wellington, Ohio, who placed it "on a spur of the Big Hill, in Jackson County, almost 13 miles from Berea" (Mallery 1893, 81). Its reported location was south of Pine Grove School on the Johnetta Quadrangle. Field reconnaissance indicated that the reported location now had a county road constructed over it. The road construction apparently destroyed the petroglyphs.

DESCRIPTION: According to Mallery (1893, 81), W. E. Barton of Wellington, Ohio, described the site in a letter written 4 October 1890. The site consisted of:

> a large rock which old settlers say was covered with soil and vegetation within their memory. Upon it are representations of human tracks, with what appear to be those of a bear, a horse, and a dog. These are all in the same direction, as though a man leading a horse, followed the dog upon the bear's track. Crossing these is a series of tracks of another and larger sort which I can not attempt to identify. The stone is a sandstone in the subcarboniferous. As I remember, the strata are nearly horizontal, but erosion has made the surface a slope of about 20°. The tracks ascending the slope cross the strata. I have not seen them for some years.
>
> The crossing of the strata shows that the tracks are the work of human hands, if indeed it were not preposterous to think of anything else in rocks of that period. Still the tracks are so well made that one is tempted to ask if they can be real. They alternate right and left, though the erosion and travel have worn out some of the left tracks. A wagon road passes over the rock and was the cause of the present exposure of the stone.

BIBLIOGRAPHIC SOURCES: Coy 1991, 1993; Mallery 1893.

LITTLE MUD CREEK PICTOGRAPH SITE (15JO3)

LOCATION: Johnson County; the site is known only by a documentary account, which placed it west of Union Church on the Paintsville Quadrangle. Elevation: about 210 m (700 ft). It is also known as the Paintsville Pictograph Site.

DESCRIPTION: The description we have on the site was provided by Funkhouser and Webb (1932, 2, 206), who received information from W.E. Connelly and Mitchell Hall:

> At the mouth of Little Mud Creek about three miles west of Paintsville is a site which attracted much attention from the early settlers because of the fact that the high sandstone cliffs were decorated with figures of turtles, rattlesnakes, bears, panthers, buffaloes and human figures, which were supposed to be the work of aborigines. This site has yielded large numbers of artifacts,

particularly flint arrowheads, tomahawks and knives. It probably represents a village site.

BIBLIOGRAPHIC SOURCES: Connelly 1910; Coy 1991, 1993; Funkhouser and Webb 1932.

UNNAMED PETROGLYPH SITE (15LW93)

LOCATION: Lewis County, south of Vanceburg, where dams were constructed on the Ohio River.

DESCRIPTION: Seven footprints, a foot apart, were reported for this site. The carvings were obliterated by dam construction (Conly 1958).

BIBLIOGRAPHIC SOURCES: Conly 1958.

UNNAMED PETROGLYPH SITE (NO NUMBER)

LOCATION: Union County, across the Ohio River from Shawneetown, Illinois.

DESCRIPTION: Cox (1875) describes this site in Kentucky in his *Geological Survey of Indiana:*

> That prehistoric races were in the habit of commemorating notable events is made manifest by the numerous carvings of human tracks and the tracks of birds and quadrupeds upon massive blocks of stone which lie at horizons which mark the lowest or highest water of large rivers. An example of this is seen at the "Foot-print rocks," in Union County, Kentucky, situated at the edge of the bottom land approaching the Shawneetown ferry. On a massive sandstone which here rises above the surface of the ground at an angle of twenty-four degrees there are a great number of carved feet of men, birds and quadrupeds, which occupy the horizon of the highest known water of the Ohio River.

Collins (1874b) also described this site: "About eight miles from Morganfield, there is a large, flat rock, with a number of deeply indented and perfectly distinct impressions of the naked feet of human beings, of all sizes, together with very plain footprints of the dog." This site was destroyed by road building.

BIBLIOGRAPHIC SOURCES: Collins 1874, vol. 2; Coy 1991, 1993; Cox 1875.

KENTUCKY PETROGLYPHS AND PICTOGRAPHS
OF EURO-AMERICAN ORIGIN

Numerous examples of carved initials, dates, and other symbols that were executed by non–Native American people were encountered over the course of this study. No systematic attempt to record such examples was undertaken. The following examples constitute a sample of sites encountered.

1. 15BL63 (CMNH-15BL1): A series of initials and geometric lines and figures on a rock in Bell County was reported by Charles Marsee.
2. CMNH-15HA1: An eagle drawn with black soot on the wall of a rock-shelter in Hancock County was reported to the Kentucky Heritage Council by Floyd Stewart of Owensboro.
3. CMNH-15HK1: Holes in a large rock under a railroad bridge near Houston in Hopkins County were reported by Mrs. Louise Renfis of Madisonville.
4. 15LO109 (CMNH-15LO1): A carved, horned animal was reported in a rockshelter on the farm of Fred Stratton of Russellville, Logan County.
5. 15LV160 (CMNH-15LV1): Carvings of a bird and a fish are visible on a slab of rock in a rockshelter less than a mile from Cave Spring Church in Livingston County.
6. 15MD16 (CMNH-15MD1): A carving of a large bird, leading to the name of "Turkey Rock" for the site, was recorded just downriver from Brandenburg in Meade County.
7. 15ML124 (CMNH-15ML1): Literature reports some carvings in rocks in the Tennessee River north of Calvert City in Marshall County. Drawings of designs on the site lead us to believe this was a Euro-American site.
8. CMNH-15MU1: This site is known from literature as the Indian Rock on Mud River in Muhlenberg County. As long ago as 1932, it was reported as Euro-American by Funkhouser and Webb (1932, 2:313–14).
9. CMNH-15OH1: Clay and ash designs were reported in the McHenry Peter Cave in Ohio County. Despite a contrary opinion from a professional archaeologist, we do not believe them to be Native American in origin.
10. CMNH-15WA1: A series of sharply cut straight lines, arrows, and circles are carved on sandstone rocks about a mile from the Green River in Warren County. These were reported to the Office of State Archaeology by Thomas T. Welborn of Alvaton, Kentucky.

4

CONCLUSIONS

The investigations of the petroglyphs and pictographs in Kentucky resulted in the compilation of numerous sites exhibiting a variety of designs and motifs. In general, these examples of Native American rock art share many similarities with other sites documented in Ohio and Pennsylvania (Swauger 1974, 1984).

The rock art sites described in this book provide the necessary data to answer many of the questions we had about the petroglyphs of Kentucky. We now know the spatial distribution of Native American petroglyphs within Kentucky. Also, considerable information has been compiled on sites that no longer exist or are not currently accessible.

Our research has demonstrated that petroglyphs were usually made by initially pecking the outline of the intended design into a rock surface. These pecked lines were then converted into grooves by abrading. Sometimes petroglyphs were made solely by pecking or abrading.

Pictographs are uncommon in the eastern United States, and Kentucky is no exception. Only two pictograph sites, where designs were painted on rock surfaces, were found during this study. One reason for the scarcity of pictographs may be weather conditions that are not conductive to the longevity of painted surfaces. Historically trees were the medium for picture writing by

Native American in the Eastern Woodland. These "dendroglyphs" were painted on tree trunks after the bark had been removed, resulting in decay of the tree and loss of the paintings.

Many difficult questions still remain to be answered. When were these carvings made? Who made them? What relationships exist between petroglyph sites and the design elements present at these sites? What can petroglyphs teach us about the men or women who made them and the societies of which they were a part? Finally, why were these carvings made? We hope further research can address some of these questions.

SPATIAL DISTRIBUTION

In his works on the petroglyphs and pictographs of the Upper Ohio Valley and Ohio, Swauger (1974, 94–98; 1984, 251–55) presented charts detailing site contents in relation to water, flowing or still, ridges, and hillsides, or flat country. For Kentucky we developed the design distributions that follow, but we did not include locales, as was done for the 1974 and 1984 Swauger works, since the listing of contents according to site locations did not prove fruitful to discussion and interpretation. Most sites studied are in hilly country, and all but two were cut into or painted on sandstone.

DESIGN CONTENT AND INTERPRETATION

Some of the following appeared in Swauger's *Rock Art of the Upper Ohio Valley* (1974, 99–112) and his *Petroglyphs of Ohio* (1984, 257–74), and thanks must be expressed to Akademische Druck- und Verlagsanstalt and the Ohio University Press for permission to reproduce here what first appeared in those two volumes.

Even with the pitfalls inherent in attempts to name a design as if we know exactly what its creator meant it to represent (Swauger 1974, 99–100; 1984, 257–58), we can make limited interpretations concerning the importance to their creators of specific design classes based on their frequency of occurrence. Classifiable designs or motifs fell within four general categories: (1) geometric, (2) animal, (3) human, and (4) miscellaneous. Only the sites listed as Native American are included in the distribution lists that follow. Excluded are the Mantle Rock petroglyphs, which, though thought to be of Native American manufacture, were probably produced in historic times.

Of the 61 Native American sites in the sample, at least 17 contain geometric motifs. These are most commonly curvilinear forms ranging from circles with varying characteristics to quite complex forms such as those at Jeffry Cliff (15HA114), Spratt's (15MF353), High Rock (15PO25), and White's (15PO154). The complex and unique quadrangles at Turkey Rock (15BT64) are another striking example of the creative energies of Native American carvers.

The following frequencies occur for specific geometric designs:

Circle and pit	3
Circle, complex interior	2
Concentric circles	4
Circle and straight line	1
Circle, exterior rays	1
Circle, interior cross	2
Complex curvilinear forms	4
Quadrangles	1
Spirals	2
TOTAL	20

Quantitative differences are notable when the contents of the 61 Kentucky sites, 27 Ohio sites, and 21 Upper Ohio Valley sites are compared. Geometric motifs occurred in all recorded upper Ohio Valley sites but were present much less often in Ohio. Kentucky fell between these two extremes with slightly more than a quarter of the recorded sites containing geometric motifs. This percentage could increase if some of the linear motifs under miscellaneous were classified as geometric.

The second major category of petroglyphs relate to animals. Most frequently, animals are represented in Kentucky petroglyphs by their tracks. The frequencies of sites calculated for each motif are as follows:

Animal tracks, unspecified	4
Bird tracks	31
Cloven hoof tracks, unspecified	3
Deer tracks	7
Elk tracks	1
Bear tracks	7
Rabbit tracks	3
Turtle	1
Raptorial/other bird	2
Insect	1
Four-legged, tailed animal	1
TOTAL	61

The predominance of bird tracks is obvious, followed by deer or other cloven hoof tracks and bear tracks. The importance of these animals in the prehistoric Native American diet is well documented in archaeological studies of faunal remains, so their strong representation comes as no surprise. The unique examples, however, are equally interesting, particularly the raptorial bird at Burnt Ridge (15MA197) and the turtle at Big Sinking Creek Turtle Rock (15LE57). The enigmatic larval-like motif from Perdue (15LE111) is also unusual.

The third general category concerns the depiction of humans in petroglyphs. As with animals, the most common representation is prints, either hand or foot, with far fewer examples of other body parts or the complete human figure. Site frequencies follow:

Hand print	2
Hand and arm	1
Footprint	15
Human head	2
Vulva form	2
Full figure	5
TOTAL	26

The depictions of full figures are intriguing. The figure at Reedyville (15BT65) is unique since it stands on a circle with an interior vertical line. The single example of a hand and arm print also occurs at this site.

One of the two pictographs recorded in Kentucky also depicts a probable human figure that appears to be wearing a mask. It is accompanied by another incomplete human figure, a small bird-like depiction and various other designs such as an hourglass-shaped motif that is part of a circular design.

Sparks Indian Rock House (15ES26) is notable for its variety of human related petroglyphs, ranging from hand- and footprints, heads, and a vulva form to a stick figure representing an entire body.

Other stick figures were recorded at Burnt Ridge (15MA197) (although one might be a lizard) and Trinity (15WO26). Burnt Ridge also included the raptorial bird design.

The Miscellaneous category includes a variety of motifs and markings that have been classified in functional terms (arrow, abrading areas/tool-sharpening grooves) or those that do not fit readily in the other categories, such as pits (occurring in isolation or in groups), pit and grooves, incised lines in various configurations ("V," "Y," and "L" shapes, for example, as well as similar forms not resembling letters), chevrons, figure 8s or zigzag linear figures. The frequency of sites for each design is as follows:

Incised lines	4
Arrow	1
Pits	2
Pit and grooves	2
Figure 8	1
Chevron	4
Zigzag linear figure	1

Swauger (1974, 99–108; 1984, 257–66) devoted considerable discussion to analytical approaches and methods of interpreting the contents of the recorded sites. His general conclusion, and it is the conclusion of the authors of this work, is that we cannot explain the meaning or the usages of the petroglyphs of Kentucky. Others are not so pessimistic. Mark F. Seeman (1986, 69), in a review of Swauger's 1984 book on Ohio rock art, suggested the use of existing statistical procedures and other forms of analysis or analogy.

At the 1987 Society for American Archaeology meetings in Toronto, two investigators suggested interpretation of sites in the general region of our interest. Jay F. Custer presented a provocative paper on petroglyph sites in the Susquehanna River Valley near Harrisburg, suggesting their origin as being Late Prehistoric Algonkian Minguannan as distinct from the archaeologically known Shanks Ferry culture and the archaeologically and ethnohistorically known Susquehannocks (Custer 1987). Thor Conway spoke of the meanings of petroglyphs in the Canadian Lake Superior region based on data collected from living informants with whom he has achieved rapport (Conway 1987).

So the possibility of interpretation of the Kentucky sites exists, and here we agree with Seeman. We are at the point where, to the best of our ability, we have presented the content of petroglyph and pictograph sites of Kentucky as a basic data set from which interpretations can be developed by others who wish to do so.

CHRONOLOGY

Kentucky rock art spans a time period from Late Archaic (1000 B.C.) to Historic. The Turkey Rock petroglyphs (15BT64) and the Asphalt pictographs (15ED24) appear to be Mississippian. Amburgy Hollow (15PO108), Nada Tunnel 2 (15PO106), and Old Landing (15LE113) petroglyphs are thought to have Fort Ancient components (Meadows 1995). The Red Bird River petroglyphs (15CY51) are reported to be Historic (Kentucky Historical Society

1969). However, the majority of the petroglyph sites fall into the Late Archaic or Woodland periods. In the Daniel Boone National Forest of Winchester, Kentucky, most of the petroglyph sites have been evaluated by a professional archaeologist. Cecil Ison, forest archaeologist for Daniel Boone, was contacted (1995) for his opinion about the age of the petroglyphs. He had available the reports that were prepared by contract archaeologists, which often included petroglyph sites, and he had visited most of the sites personally. Ison stated that the bulk of the sites in Daniel Boone had diagnostics that were of the Late Archaic or Early Woodland periods. A few of the multiple component sites had late prehistoric diagnostics, but when they did the late prehistoric diagnostics were few. At a number of the petroglyph sites, bedrock mortars were found. These are generally regarded as being associated with the Cogswell phase, again, during the Late Archaic and Woodland periods. According to Ison there appears to be a belt in eastern Kentucky, north of the Kentucky River, and in western Kentucky, from the Green River to the Ohio, that establishes a correlation between petroglyph sites and the occurrence of bedrock mortars.

Both Swauger (1974, 108–9; 1984, 267–69) and Custer (1987) concluded that petroglyphs studied in Ohio, West Virginia, and Pennsylvania were created during the late prehistoric period (A.D. 900–1600). Swauger finds that the Kentucky sites are sufficiently similar to those of Ohio, Pennsylvania, and West Virginia to suggest a late prehistoric origin.

CULTURAL ORIGIN

Although in the past Swauger advanced the suggestion that some, at least, of the rock art of Ohio, Pennsylvania, and West Virginia was produced by proto-Shawnee inhabitants of those areas (Swauger 1974, 109; 1984, 269), and even though the Shawnee were intimately connected with Kentucky as a homeland, we here do not name a specific proto-historic or historic Native American tribe as responsible for the rock art production. We adhere to the belief that the rock art was produced by local native groups but do not feel that a tribal name or names can be assigned.

RELATIONSHIPS TO OTHER PETROGLYPH SITES AND DESIGNS

As intimated in discussions above, Swauger finds reason to believe that as a group the petroglyphs and pictographs of Kentucky are the products of a late prehistoric people. They are of a "northeastern" character associated with Algonkian speaking peoples (Mallery 1893, 45–46) as manifested in petroglyphs studied by Swauger in the New England states (except for the very northern reaches of Maine), the Mid-Atlantic states, Virginia, West Virginia, and now Kentucky. The reasoning leading to this conclusion is set forth at length in Swauger's 1974 and 1984 publications. Essentially, the Kentucky designs more closely resemble petroglyphs and pictographs of the northeast United States rather than the southeast or western parts of the country.

The unique aspect about many of the Kentucky petroglyph sites is the relationship between the track motif and the bedrock mortars. As a matter of fact, many of the sites consist only of track motifs. This in itself puts the sites in a different category than many others of the eastern United States. True, the track motif is ubiquitous, but elsewhere tracks most often occur with other motifs.

In general, the designs of the sites in Kentucky were well-executed. The bird tracks and turtle of Big Sinking Creek Turtle Rock (15LE57), the "Meso-American style" complicated design on the smaller rock of High Rock (15PO25), and the many complicated designs of Turkey Rock (15BT64) are evidence of considerable skill in planning and execution. Consensus among the four of us is their creators were careful craftsmen for the most part and that the work they did was important to them, whether as art or in connection with religious rituals such as sympathetic magic. We believe there is little evidence in the Kentucky sites of idle scratching. Beyond these speculations, however, we cannot presently go.

It is the opinion of at least one of the authors that an attempt to categorize and group these Kentucky petroglyphs must be approached with a great deal of caution. Certain characteristics may easily relate these sites to those in the surrounding geographical regions. Other characteristics make the Kentucky sites unique. For instance, fifteen of the sites contain bedrock mortars with associated animal tracks (including human footprints). None of these sites show any encroachment of the petroglyphs on the mortar holes or mortar hole encroachment on the petroglyphs. This is not reported in any of the surrounding states. The bedrock mortars, which are so common in Kentucky north of the Kentucky and Green Rivers, are not found in any abundance in any of the other surrounding states. Our archaeological friends tell us that these particular sites probably date to the Terminal Archaic period. On the other hand the sites along the Green River have every indication of being Mississippian, and the Asphalt (15ED24) pictograph may actually be Historic and related to the Great Lake cultures.

Most of the Kentucky petroglyphs are on rather loosely cemented, porous, Pennsylvanian sandstones with friable surfaces. The petroglyphs are attacked both physically and chemically—physically by freezing, thawing, and wind abrasion and chemically by environmental acids. The petroglyphs that are out in the open are subject to attack by plants, such as lichens, algae, and the rootlets of vascular plants. Perhaps the most destructive forces are due to the dissolved salts in the sandstone, which are carried through the porous sandstone to the surface. Here they are concentrated, which is both good and bad. They do give the surface a type of case hardening that affords some protection. But as the salts (potassium nitrate and calcium sulfate have frequently been found along with some of the iron salts) are collected, the precipitated crystals tend to expand and by so doing erode the surface. Fortunately this erosion occurs all across the surface of the sandstone, one grain of sand at time. As a result the petroglyphs recede into the sandstone, somewhat blunted but retaining the design elements. However, because of this the surface is constantly being renewed, so any attempt to date this rock art is fraught with difficulty. At the present time, we must rely on relating the carvings to the associated midden, which may or may not have any relationship. Also, generally the midden has been so disrupted by collectors of artifacts that it is virtually worthless as a dating tool. Indirect methods, such as comparing the petroglyph motifs with design elements on datable portable artifacts, is at the present time the method of choice.

Finally, we come to the question of searching out the meaning or interpreting the petroglyphs. Unless we are able to put ourselves in the place of the artist making the petroglyph, we will never know what he or she was thinking and can only speculate. (Today it is even difficult to know what is in the mind of the perpetrators of modern-day graffiti.) Petroglyphs are only a small corner of the puzzle. We know from the early journals that dendroglyphs (Johnson 1898, 155; Schoolcraft 1851, 333–40) were perhaps the most important and widespread media to express their art. Trying to extract a meaning from present-day descendants of Native Americans is also quite difficult, as many of the petroglyphs and pictographs date from the Terminal Archaic or Early Woodland period. The continuity of individual groups, of course, no longer exists. Even in areas where the Native Americans can trace their ancestors for many generations, an informant may tailor his or her stories to fit the current times or the suggestions of the interviewer.

We believe the rock art we have presented to be of Native American origin based on the homogeneity of the designs in sites of the northeastern United States. We find no reason to accept the opinion of some that such sites as Old Landing (15LE113) and Amburgy Hollow (15PO108) were carved by pre-Columbian visitors from Europe, as is claimed for similar sites in the northeastern United States (Fell 1976; 1978; 1980).

These petroglyphs and pictographs are one very fragile remnant that links us with Kentucky's past. They should be protected, and the public should be informed of their importance at every opportunity. Research using state-of-the-art techniques should be encouraged with the involvement of many disciplines. The rocks have a lot to tell us if we are patient and do not destroy them either through neglect or through misplaced loving care.

abrade To remove the rock matrix by rubbing with another tool of harder material.

bear track A petroglyph characterized by a circular motif representing the footpad and smaller circular motifs arranged in an arc outside the larger circle and representing toes.

bird track A petroglyph motif characterized by three lines emanating from a single point, forward and frequently one line to the rear, to form a fan-like configuration similar to the print of a toed bird such as a turkey.

BM Abbreviation for "bench mark," found on all topographic maps. Bench mark is defined as a relatively permanent metal tablet or other mark firmly embedded in a fixed and enduring natural or artificial object, indicating a precisely determined elevation above or below a standard datum (usually sea level), bearing identifying information, and used as a reference in topographic surveys.

deer track A petroglyph motif characterized by two oval motifs representing toes, sometimes with two small circles beneath, representing dewclaws.

dendroglyph Picture writing or paintings on the trunks of trees stripped of their bark.

elk track A petroglyph motif having the same appearance as a deer track but being larger in size.

hominy hole A cylindrical hole in sandstone, commonly interpreted as having been used prehistorically for grinding foodstuffs; synonymous with bedrock mortar.

incise To carve with a sharp tool that leaves a U-shaped or V-shaped cross-section; synonymous with carve.

peck To strike a rock surface with a sharp or pointed tool, frequently the first step in creating the outline of a petroglyph.

rockshelter A sheltered overhang in a cliffline formed when less resistant rock erodes beneath a more resistant rock formation; colloquially referred to as a "rock house."

vulva form A V-shaped motif that may represent human female genitalia.

Brownlee, Richard S. 1956. The Big Moniteau Bluff Pictographs in Boone County, Missouri. *Missouri Archaeologist* 18(4):49–56.

Burroughs, Wilbur Greeley. 1938a. Footprints Found in Ages-Old Stone. *New York Times,* 20 January.

———. 1938b. Burroughs to Waldemar Kaempffert, science editor, *New York Times.*

———. 1940. Fossil Tracks in Eastern Kentucky. *Kentucky Academy of Science Transactions* 8:14.

Bushnell, David I., Jr. 1913. Petroglyphs Representing the Imprint of the Human Foot. *American Anthropologist* n.s. 15:8–15.

Caldwell, Joseph R. 1958. *Trend and Tradition in the Prehistory of the Eastern United States.* Memoir 88. American Anthropological Association.

Cambron, J.W., and S.A. Waters. 1959. Petroglyphs and Pictographs in the Tennessee Valley and Surrounding Area. *Journal of Alabama Archaeology* 5(2):26–51.

Collins, Richard H. 1874. *History of Kentucky.* 2 vols. Reprint, Kentucky Historical Society, Frankfort, 1966.

Conly, Ralph. 1958. Column on the River. *Intelligencer* (Wheeling, W.Va.), 28 July.

Connelley, William Elsey. 1910. *The Founding of Harman's Station with an Account of the Indian Captivity of Mrs. Jenny Wiley and the Exploration and Settlement of the Big Sandy Valley in the Virginias and Kentucky.* New York: Torch Press.

Conway, Thor. 1987. Shamanic Rituals and the Interpretation of Ojibwa Rock Art. Paper delivered at the 52d Annual Meeting of the Society for American Archaeology, Toronto, Canada.

Cox, E.T. 1875. *Sixth Annual Report of the Geological Survey of Indiana, Made during the Year of 1874.* Indianapolis: Sentinel Co.

Coy, Fred E., Jr. 1966. Rock Carvings in Kentucky. *Bulletin of the Jefferson County Medical Society* 14(6):16–17, Louisville.

———. 1991. The Accounts and Recordings of Aboriginal Petroglyphs and Pictographs Occurring within the Boundaries of the Commonwealth of Kentucky. In *Studies in Kentucky Archaeology,* ed. Charles D. Hockensmith, 152–63. Frankfort: Kentucky Heritage Council.

———. 1993. Petroglyphs and Pictographs in Kentucky. Paper delivered at the Eastern States Rock Art Conference, Natural Bridge, Kentucky.

———. 1994. Two Cases of Mistaken Identity. Paper delivered at the International Rock Art Congress, Flagstaff, Arizona.

Coy, Fred E., Jr., and Thomas C. Fuller. 1966. Petroglyphs of North Central Kentucky. *Tennessee Archaeologist* 22(2):53–66.

———. 1967. Turkey Rock Petroglyphs, Green River, Kentucky. *Tennessee Archaeologist* 23(2):58–79.

———. 1968. Tar Springs Petroglyphs, Breckinridge County, Kentucky. *Tennessee Archaeologist* 24(1): 29–35.

———. 1969a. The Asphalt Pictograph, Edmonson County, Kentucky. *Tennessee Archaeologist* 25(2):37–46.

———. 1969b. Red Bird River Petroglyphs, Clay County, Kentucky. *Southeastern Archaeological Conference Newsletter* 10:27–31.

———. 1970a. Reedyville Petroglyphs, Butler County, Kentucky. *Central States Archaeological Journal* 17(3):100–109.

———. 1970b. Outline of Thoughts on Kentucky Petroglyphs. Presentation given at the Eastern States Archeological Federation Symposium on Petroglyphs in the Eastern United States, Natural Bridge, Virginia.

———. 1971. Petroglyphs of Powell County, Kentucky. *Central States Archaeological Journal* 18(3):112–22.

Custer, Jay F. 1987. Patterns in Petroglyphs and in Ceramics of the Lower Susquehanna Valley. Paper delivered at the 52d Annual Meeting of the Society for American Archaeology, Toronto, Canada.

Diesing, E.H., and F. Magre. 1942. Petroglyphs and Pictographs in Missouri. *Missouri Archaeologist* 8(1):8–18.

Fell, Barry. 1976. *America B.C.: Ancient Settlers in the New World*. New York: Pocket Books.

———. 1978. Vermont's Ancient Sites and the Larger Picture of Trans-Atlantic Visitations to America, B.C. In *Ancient Vermont,* ed. Warren L. Cook, 70–84. Castleton, Vt.: Castleton State College.

———. 1980. *Saga America*. New York: New York Times Books.

Fuller, Thomas C. 1969a. Ancient Picture Writing in Kentucky. *Happy Hunting Ground* 25(5):15–18.

———. 1969b. Ancient Carvings on Banks of Green River. *Ohio County Messenger* (Beaver Dam, Ky), March 14.

———. 1985. Personal communication with Tom Fuller in regard to his visit to the Wickliffe Petroglyphs site.

Funkhouser, W.D., and W.S. Webb. 1929. The So-Called "Ash Caves" in Lee County, Kentucky. *Reports in Archaeology and Anthropology* (Department of Anthropology and Archaeology, University of Kentucky), 1(2):37–112.

———. 1930. Rock Shelters of Wolfe and Powell Counties. *Reports in Archaeology and Anthropology* 4:239–306.

———. 1932. Archaeological Survey of Kentucky. *Reports in Archaeology and Anthropology* 2:411.

Hall, Mitchel. 1928. *Johnson County Kentucky: A History of the County and Genealogy of Its People up to the Year 1927*. Vol. 1. Louisville, Ky.: Standard Press.

Haynes, Col. William R. 1876. *Dock Brown: The Outlaw of Grayson County*. Reprint, Leitchfield, Ky: *Leitchfield Gazette,* 1950.

Hockensmith, Charles D. 1981. Kentucky Archaeological Site Survey Form for 15Bt40, Butler County. On file at the Office of State Archaeology, Lexington.

Ison, Cecil. 1995. Telephone conversation of Cecil Ison, Daniel Boone National Forest archaeologist, Winchester, Ky., with Fred E. Coy Jr., 21–22 August.

Jobe, Cynthia, Malinda Stafford, and Richard Boisvert. 1980. An Archaeological Survey and Assessment of Various Timber Sale Areas, Road Rights-of-Way and Land Exchanges within the Daniel Boone National Forest. Report submitted to the U.S. Forest Service, Daniel Boone National Forest, Winchester, Ky. *Archaeological Report* (Department of Anthropology, University of Kentucky), 29:111–32.

Johnson, J. Stoddard. 1898. *First Explorations of Kentucky: Doctor Thomas Walker's Journal and Colonel Christopher Gist's Journal.* Filson Club Publication No. 13. Louisville, Ky.: John P. Morton.

Jonaitis, Aldona. 1981. Tlingit Halibut Hooks: An Analysis of the Visual Symbols of a Rite of Passage. *Anthropological Papers of the American Museum of Natural History* (New York) 57, part 1.

Kentucky Historical Society. 1969. *Guide of Kentucky Historical Highway Markers.* Frankfort: Kentucky Historical Society.

Kingery, W.D. 1982. Report to Fred E. Coy Jr. from Dr. Kingery, Professor of Ceramics, Massachusetts Institute of Technology, on the analysis of the pigment from the Asphalt Pictograph Site (15ED24).

Knudsen, Gary D. 1980. Archaeological Survey of Impact Area on the Daniel Boone National Forest. U.S. Forest Service, Daniel Boone National Forest, Winchester, Ky.

Knudsen, Gary D., and S. Simpson. 1982. Site Survey Form for Big Sinking Creek Turtle Rock Petroglyphs Site (15LE57). Copy on file, Office of State Archaeology, University of Kentucky.

Kroeber, A.L. 1963. *Cultural and Natural Areas of Native North America.* Berkeley: University of California Press.

Lee, Georgia. 1991. *Rock Art and Cultural Resource Management.* Calabasas, Calif.: Wormwood Press.

Loughridge, R.H. 1888. *Report on the Geological and Economic Features of the Jackson's Purchase Region, Embracing the Counties of Ballard, Calloway, Fulton, Graves, Hickman, McCracken, and Marshall, Kentucky.* Frankfort: Geological Survey of Kentucky.

McMurtrie, Henry. 1819. *Sketches of Louisville and its Environs.* Louisville, Ky.: S. Penn.

Mallery, Garrick. 1893. Picture-Writing of the American Indians. *Tenth Annual Report, Bureau of American Ethnology.* Washington, D.C.: Smithsonian Institution.

Meadows, Larry. 1995. Telephone conversation of Larry Meadows, Powell County, Ky., with Fred E. Coy Jr., 22 August.

Moore, C.B. 1916. Some Aboriginal Sites on Green River, Kentucky. *Journal of the Academy of Natural Sciences of Philadelphia* (2d Series) 16(3):431–92.

Murphy, James L. 1969. Note on Tar Burner Rocks. *Ohio Archaeologist* 19(4):115–17.

O'Steen, Lisa D., Kristen J. Gremillion, and R. Jerald Ledbeetter. 1991. Archaeological Testing of Five Sites in the Big Sinking Creek Oil Field, Lee County, Kentucky.

Report submitted to the U.S. Forest Service, Daniel Boone National Forest, Winchester, Ky.

Parker, M. 1948. Study of the Rocky Green Pictograph. *Tennessee Archaeologist* 5(2):13–17.

Peithman, Irvin. 1952. Pictographs and Petroglyphs in Southern Illinois. *Journal of the Illinois State Archaeological Society* (Springfield) 2(4): 91–94.

Rothert, Otto A. 1913. *History of Muhlenberg County.* Louisville, Ky.: John P. Morton.

Sanders, Thomas N. 1977. Kentucky Prehistoric Resources Inventory Form for Pilot Rock. Copy on file, Office of State Archaeology, University of Kentucky.

Sanders, Thomas N., and David R. Maynard. 1979. *A Reconnaissance and Evaluation of Archaeological Sites in Christian County, Kentucky.* Survey Report 12. Frankfort: Kentucky Heritage Commission.

Schoolcraft, Henry R. 1851. *Information Respecting the History Condition and Prospects of the Indian Tribes of the United States.* Part 1. Collected and prepared under the direction of the Bureau of Indian Affairs. Philadelphia: Lippincott, Grambo.

Schwartz, Douglas W. 1960. An Archaeological Survey of the Nolin River Reservoir. Manuscript on file at the Office of State Archaeology, University of Kentucky.

Seeman, Mark F. 1986. Review of "Petroglyphs of Ohio" (1984). *Pennsylvania Archaeologist* 56(3–4): 68–69.

Shawe, Fred E. 1966. *Geologic Map of the Reedyville Quadrangle, Western Kentucky.* Washington, D.C.: U.S. Geological Survey.

Squier, E.G., and E.H. Davis. 1848. *Ancient Monuments of the Mississippi Valley: Comprising the Results of Extensive Original Surveys and Explorations.* Washington, D.C.: Smithsonian Institution.

Stoltman, James B. 1978. Temporal Models in Prehistory: An Example from Eastern North America. *Current Anthropology* 19(4):703–46.

Swauger, James L. 1960. The Bunola Head—A Forgery. *Pennsylvania Archaeologist* 30(2):63–64.

———. 1961. Techniques of Petroglyph Recording. *Eastern States Archaeological Federation Bulletin* 20:14–15.

———. 1974. *Rock Art of the Upper Ohio Valley.* Akademische Druck-und Verlagsanstalt, Graz, Austria.

———. 1978. The "Lost" Petroglyph Rock of the Barnesville Track Rocks Petroglyphs Rock. *Pennsylvania Archaeologist* 48(1–2): 53–54.

———. 1980. Grooved Rock Petroglyph Sites as Tool-Sharpening and Polishing Locations. *Arkansas Archaeologist* 21:29–33.

———. 1984. *Petroglyphs of Ohio.* Athens: Ohio University Press.

Turnbow, Christopher A., Melinda Stafford, Richard Boisvert, and Julie Reisenweber. 1980. A Cultural Resource Assessment of Two Alternate Locations the Hancock Power Plant, Hancock and Breckinridge Counties, Kentucky. Report submitted to Kentucky Utilities Company, Lexington. *Archaeological Report* (Department of Anthropology, University of Kentucky) 30.

Weber, J. Cynthia. 1971. Analogies, Hypotheses, and Grooved Rocks. *Arkansas Archeologist* 12(3):53–55.

Weinland, Marcia K., and Thomas N. Sanders. 1977. Reconnaissance and Evaluation of Archaeological Sites in Powell County, Kentucky. *Kentucky Heritage Commission Reports* (Frankfort) 3.

Weller, James Marvin. 1927. *The Geology of Edmonson County.* Frankfort: Kentucky Geological Survey.

Wellman, Klaus F. 1979. *A Survey of North American Indian Rock Art.* Graz, Austria: Akademische Druck- und Verlagsanstalt.

Wentworth, W.A. 1969. Letter to Dr. Fred E. Coy Jr., 20 November.

Wyss, James D., and Sandra K. Wyss. 1977. An Archaeological Assessment of Portions of the Red River Gorge Geological Area, Menifee County, Kentucky. Report prepared by the University of Kentucky Museum of Anthropology, Lexington.

Note: Page numbers in *italics* refer to figures.